MARTHA CULBERTSON
& REBECCA FARNBACH

FLAVORS

of the Temecula Valley Wineries

MARTHA CULBERTSON
& REBECCA FARNBACH

FLAVORS

of the Temecula Valley Wineries

WITH PHOTOGRAPHS BY
JOHNNY C. VELASQUEZ

WITH CULINARY ASSISTANCE BY
JEAN VESEY

PUBLISHED BY GREAT OAK PRESS
PECHANGA, CALIFORNIA

Published in 2023 by Great Oak Press, Pechanga, California.

Photographs by Johnny C. Velasquez, Johhny C. Photography.

ISBN: 978-1-942279-36-5 (Hardcover)
ISBN: 978-1-942279-38-9 (Ebook)

Library of Congress Control Number: 2023939963

Front Cover: Photo by Johnny C. Velasquez, Johhny C. Photography. A special thank you to Wilson Creek Winery & Vineyards for allowing us to stage this beautiful dining scene in their vineyard.

For updates and current news about this book, follow us on Facebook at www.facebook.com/FlavorsTVW.

For more information visit www.greatoakpress.com.

Printed in Canada by TC Transcontinental.

Great Oak Press
P.O. Box 1477
Temecula, CA, 92593
United States of America

We dedicate this book to the pioneers who came to work the soil and invest funds to make Temecula a wine lovers' destination, with special recognition to Ely Calloway, Vincenzo and Audrey Cilurzo, and John Culbertson. You had a vision and worked to make it happen, planting vineyards, opening tasting rooms, and marketing the Temecula dream that came true.

CONTENTS

Our first vineyard adventure for our book. Many have seen vines at their best, when the branches are adorned with grapes. Few get the opportunity to appreciate the raw beauty and complexities of the dormant stage of the vines. Wilson Creek Winery & Vineyards, December 6, 2018.

PREFACE

On most days, a thick marine layer blanket shrouds Interstate 15, parting just south of Rancho California Road, revealing the Valley's lush hills and granite mountains. To the west lies the Rainbow Gap, which allows marine breezes to cool Temecula Valley's vineyards to the east. These marine breezes provide a welcoming climate for growing grapes in a region that would otherwise be too hot for successful wine grape growing.

The vision for this book was originally conceptualized by Martha Culbertson. As if destined to be, Martha would suggest the concept for the cookbook and ask Rebecca Farnbach to coauthor the book over lunch at Journey's End, a restaurant owned by the Pechanga Band of Indians, who as it turns out, also established Pechanga's Great Oak Press, the publisher of this cookbook. Rebecca, a historian, writer, and lover of books, happily accepted the role of coauthor. Together, Martha and Rebecca have over sixty years of experience in Southern California's Temecula Valley. Rebecca is among the few, other than the Indigenous peoples of the valley, who know the valley's most intimate secrets. Martha, a food and wine pioneer, together with Ely Callaway, Vincenzo Cilurzo, Audrey Cilurzo, and John Culbertson was instrumental in turning Temecula into a wine lovers' destination.

Like planting the first vineyards in the valley, creating this cookbook was a considerable undertaking and not without its challenges. Wednesdays became our cooking days in Martha's home. Much of the serving ware you see in this book, was generously loaned from friends and family. Jean Vesey, a close friend and student of Martha's assisted in the kitchen. Martha and Jean prepared five to six delectable dishes each week that were photographed by Johnny Velasquez and sampled by all. For over six months, Martha's home was converted into a quasi-commercial kitchen and photography studio.

The other days of the week were just as busy. Mondays were for grocery shopping, Tuesdays for prep, and the other days were filled with attending meetings with winery owners, vineyard managers, and winemakers, as well as, coordinating with the photographer, whom as you can see from the photographs, perfectly captured the abundant flavors and beauty of the Temecula Valley Appellation. The last photoshoot took place at Wilson Creek Winery & Vineyards. The team staged a rustic table with dishes and wine selections from the book. It was a celebratory event, the weather holding out just long enough to take the last photo before it started raining.

With over one hundred recipes and thousands of photographs to sort through, organizing the book would be a huge undertaking. The authors did not want this book to be "just another cookbook" with appetizers, soups and salads, entrées, side dishes, and desserts, but rather an exploration of the wineries themselves. Hence this book is organized quite differently than most cookbooks. Each section or chapter begins with a winery story, arranged alphabetically and written so eloquently by Rebecca, followed by the recipes and wine pairings from that winery. Martha scrupulously paired each wine to her recipes, selecting those she felt would balance and brighten the flavors in both the recipe and the wine. Martha also kept the readers of this book in mind when making her selections. She wanted to ensure the wines would be available and the wineries would continue producing these wines for years to come. This proved to be especially challenging. The wines in this book are as unique as the wineries, winery owners, and winemakers themselves. The recipes tell a story all their own and are equally varied — a reflection of the many cultures and cuisines Martha has come across in her worldly travels.

Unfortunately, the pandemic halted publication. Like many industries, the publishing industry was not immune to office closures, furloughs, and supply shortages. Everyone was asked to remain patient as the world sorted itself out. The authors and Great Oak Press are pleased to bring you this long overdue completed study titled, *Flavors of the Temecula Valley Wineries*. Our hope is this book will bring you the reader, home cook, chef, student, wine connoisseur, historian, and everyone in between as much joy as we had creating it.

ACKNOWLEDGMENTS

We are grateful to the owners and staff at each winery who opened their doors and their hearts to embrace this book project. We couldn't have done this without you. We want to give special thanks to Greg Pennyroyal for sharing his insights into the cycle of growth in the vineyards. And, we would like to thank Joan Gair and Catherine Harrison for loaning some of the pretty dishes featured in our photos.

We thank Great Oak Press for extending a contract to us and taking a chance on this book that is a departure from their normal topics. We couldn't have had a better editor than Lauren Niezgodzki who not only did the job of an editor, but also gave her heart and soul to the design of the pages, and even rolled up her sleeves to help wash dishes during our cooking sessions. We thank Johnny Velasquez for his artistry with food photography. Jean Vesey receives our love and thanks for her tireless help in the kitchen.

We thank the Temecula Valley Winegrowers Association and Phil Baily, TVWA President of the Board, for inducting wine country pioneers John and Martha Culbertson into the Temecula Valley Winegrowers Association Hall of Fame. John and Martha were recognized for their dedication to the promotion and growth of Temecula Valley's Wine Country.

We thank you, readers, for believing in the value of this volume, and hope it will provide you with joy as you peruse the book and taste some of the recipes we've chosen for your enjoyment.

Mission grapes, the oldest vines in the valley, planted between 1882 and 1905. From this vineyard, Hart Winery bottled and sold Angelica, as well as Old Vine Zinfandel, the first winery to do so since the 1930s. In the background, notice a thick marine layer blankets the valley. Marine breezes provide a welcoming climate for growing grapes in a region that would otherwise be too hot. Pechanga Reservation, December 6, 2018.

A HISTORY OF TEMECULA VALLEY WINERIES

BY REBECCA FARNBACH

HOW DOES A REGION GO FROM UNPLANTED AND UNKNOWN TO BEING NAMED BY WINE ENTHUSIAST MAGAZINE ONE OF THE TOP TEN WINE DESTINATIONS OF THE WORLD IN 50 YEARS?

When Lief Erickson landed in what is now known as Newfoundland a thousand years ago, he called the new land *Vineland*. He saw the land covered with vines bearing berries and believed the continent was one vast vineyard. Horticulturalists today say the fruits he saw were squash berries, also known as low bush cranberries, with leaves resembling grape leaves. Erickson was correct that much of North America is well suited for growing grapes, especially in the areas between 30 to 50 degrees south or north latitude. Of the eight species of wine grapes in the world, six are native to North America.

As for our California grape history, it starts with the Spanish explorers and missionaries to the "New World". When the explorer Hernán Cortés arrived in Mexico in 1519, he declared the wild grapes were useless for wine, brandy, or even for eating. They were probably small, dry, and full of seeds as most uncultivated fruits are.

In the 1530s Spanish padres tried to plant European vines with little success, which was a problem because the missions needed grapes to make sacramental wine as well as table wine. Several attempts were made to carry vines from Spain, but none of the root stock took well to the new climate. After many decades with several missionaries trying, Padre Juan María de Salvatierra is credited with the planting of the first successful vineyard in the Americas at the Misión de Nuestra Señora de Loreto Conchó in Baja California. It is believed that Father Junípero Serra planted the first grapes for cultivation in Alta California in 1773, from grapes he brought from Baja California missions.

Padre Juan Crespí first recorded seeing wild grapes near San Juan Capistrano and Los Angeles on his travels in 1776. The first record of sacramental wine being made in California was in 1781 in San Juan Capistrano.

During this time the eastern colonies of the United States had cultivated some vines, but grape production was limited by the short growing season and too much rain. Hard ciders and liquors were libations of choice in that region during that time.

By 1796 most California wines came from the Mission San Gabriel Arcángel. The Mission grape varietal was not well regarded because it produced red wine with a weak color, dull flavor, and low acid content. When skins were removed for making white wines, the juice looked yellow and then when oxidized, it turned an unappetizing color of brown.

There were a handful of wine entrepreneurs in the Los Angeles area. Antonio Lugo planted eight acres of several thousand vines in Los Angeles in 1809. By 1817 Los Angeles was called the "City of Vineyards" with 54,000 vines on about 60 acres. That was all before Jean-Louis Vignes arrived in Los Angeles, or its more official name, *El Pueblo de Nuestra Señora la Reina de los Ángeles Del Río Porciúncula*. Vignes took winemaking to a new level in the Americas.

Vignes is of special interest to the Temecula Valley, but he had an interesting history before his affiliation with our wine country. Vignes was born in the Bordeaux region of France where every landowner grew grapes and made wine. Vignes learned barrel making from his father who was a cooper by trade. Vignes also helped tend the family vines and make wine.

After Vignes married, he owned land with a wine cellar, vines, and a copper brandy still. He was a prominent member of the community until he had some financial problems and a disagreement with people in power, prompting him to leave France quickly and alone in 1826.

He traveled with some missionaries to the Sandwich Islands, now known as Hawaii, and engaged in making rum, which was lucrative until Queen Lydia Kamakaeha banned all alcohol production and sales.

He left Hawaii and sailed to Monterrey, California and where he registered his name as Juan-Luis Vignes (Californians pronounced it VIN-yess with a Spanish twist), and he listed his occupation as cooper and distiller. By 1831 he was in Los Angeles. He bought some land along the Los Angeles River, near present-day Alameda and Aliso Streets on the road to San Bernardino. Part of his land was where Union Station is now, near Olvera Street and Chinatown.

He planted the El Aliso Vineyard there, naming it for the landmark tree on the property. Aliso is the Spanish word for "alder", as the tree was called, but the huge tree was actually a sycamore. The tree stood 60 feet high and spread in a 200-foot diameter. His 104-acre property was noted for its quarter-mile arbor of grapes, 35 additional acres planted in grapes with more than 40,000 vines, and a wine cellar near the big tree.

Vignes, also known as Don Luis del Aliso, wanted better grapes, so he imported Cabernet Franc and Sauvignon Blanc vines from France that were shipped around Cape Horn to Los Angeles. To keep the vines alive during the journey, they were placed in containers of moss and potato slices.

His wines made their mark in California. By 1827 Vignes was the first to grow quality vines and was the first to age wines. Prior to that time, Californians drank wine right after it fermented. He aged his wines in oak barrels he made by hand from trees on land he owned in the San Bernardino Mountains.

Vignes made French-style aged Angelica and brandy. Brandy, *aguardiente* in Spanish, is a distilled wine aged in barrels with a high alcohol content usually served after dinner. Angelica is a sweet dessert wine and brandy mixture said to be named for Los Angeles where it originated. Vignes aged his Angelicas for eight years.

Vignes became the most important winemaker in the West, the first commercial winemaker in California and one of first to import and plant European grapes in California. El Aliso produced about 150,000 gallon-bottles per year. Vignes sold white wine for two dollars a gallon and brandy for four dollars a gallon.

Because Vignes made an excess supply of wine, more than could be consumed in Los Angeles, he was the first recorded Californian to ship wine. He regularly shipped to eager markets in Santa Barbara, Monterey and San Francisco. His were considered the first commercial sales of wine in California.

While Vignes was enjoying the success of his Los Angeles vineyards, he also purchased two Mexican land grants in the Temecula Valley. He bought Rancho Temecula in 1846 and Pauba Rancho in 1848. Rancho Temecula, which he owned, and the adjacent Little Temecula Rancho owned by Pablo Apis were already planted in vines, but on the Pauba Rancho, where our Temecula Wine Country is now, there is no indication of any vines in existence before or during the time Vignes owned it. Vignes sold both ranchos in 1853, perhaps without ever visiting the land. A hired caretaker watched over his ranchos for him.

An advertisement in the Elsinore Transcript newspaper in 1888 declared, "The Pauba Rancho: Grapes grow in this valley and all over the foothills wherever they have been tried, to a remarkable degree of perfection". That is our Wine Country.

It is an irony that Jean-Louis Vignes, whose surname is French for "vines" and who was the most successful person in the early California wine industry, actually owned the Pauba Rancho, the home to our Temecula Wine Country. To our knowledge, Vignes never planted vines on his land in the Temecula area. We suppose that he must have recognized how well-suited the soil and climate would be for grapes and wonder why he didn't plant here.

During the brief time Vignes owned the land near Temecula that was destined to become vineyards, cultivation of grapes for winemaking in California was a rudimentary process and there were few vintners in California who were experienced with European style winemaking. California grapes left a lot to be desired, yet he navigated through the challenges and was a forerunner for our Southern California grape growing and winemaking today.

So, how did the Temecula Wine Country go from unplanted and unknown to being named by *Wine Enthusiast* magazine as One of the Top Ten Wine Destinations in the World in just 50 years?

A number of factors enhanced the success of Temecula Wine Country. The climate is conducive to excellent grape growing with warm afternoons and cool nights, a long, dry growing season with rainfall during the early stages of vine growth. The granite-alluvial mix of rock and soil gives ample drainage and a perfect concentration of minerals that are perfectly adapted to growing a wide variety of wine grapes. And, it sits in an optimal position, at 33 degrees latitude.

Early on, dedicated vineyard managers and winemakers knew how to grow good grapes and to make excellent wine. They did their homework and stayed connected to experts here and at the University of California at Davis. Ely Callaway, a born promoter, was here in the infancy of our wine country and made some extraordinary moves to put Temecula wines on the map.

Wine had dipped in popularity during the period of Prohibition from 1920 to 1933, while there was a nationwide ban on the production, importation, transportation, and sale of alcoholic beverages, except for sacramental or medicinal purposes.

Even after the restrictions of Prohibition were lifted, a negative attitude lingered regarding alcohol consumption, as a subtly imposed national guilt. As air travel to Europe became more available, Americans became reacquainted with genteel dining and fine wines. Then Julia Child tipped the balance in 1961 when her book *Mastering the Art of French Cooking* encouraged tasty food and good wine as part of everyday life. With Julia's recommendation and the guilt alcohol consumption lifted, Americans began to savor creative cuisines paired with delicious wines.

There was early success with home winemaking in the Temecula area. The Escalliers, a family that migrated from France, owned a house and barn in Temecula where the city hall stands now. In the early 1900s the Escallier barn on Main Street, now relocated to south Pujol Street, was the winery and wine cellar for grapes they grew on their property, land that is now under lanes of Interstate 15.

Several other local families tell about trips their predecessors undertook to bring vines from France or Italy in the 1880s, planting each vine in a potato to keep the vines alive during the long journey back to California.

Felipe Cazas of Pechanga was one who went to Europe for vines. He had an establishment on Pala Road in the early 1900s where he sold wine made from his vineyards. His Mission and Zinfandel grapes are still used in some of the local wines today.

Except for the Pechanga Reservation and Old Town Temecula, the Vail Cattle Company dominated the Temecula Valley from 1904 through 1964, grazing cattle in the brush lands. When Kaiser Aetna purchased 87,500 acres from the Vail Company, they designated much of the former Pauba Rancho as citrus and grape growing areas.

In 1967 Vincenzo and Audrey Cilurzo purchased land that Vignes once owned to start a commercial vineyard. Dick Break, a viticulture expert with many years of experience in Northern California, had done a feasibility study that convinced him that Temecula's climate was equal to Napa's for growing premium varietal wine grapes. Break supervised Leon Borel as he planted vineyards of Petite Sirah and Chenin Blanc grapes on Cilurzo's land along the unpaved Long Valley Road, vineyards now owned by Maurice Car'rie Vineyard and Winery on Rancho California Road.

The University of California at Riverside's Agricultural Extension had successful plantings in the Santa Rosa Plateau, on Buck Mesa, in Lake Village, on Los Caballos, at Keyways, and at the present Twisted Tendrils location.

Shortly afterward, Philo Biane, a vintner from Rancho Cucamonga identified the Temecula area climate favorable for grapes and he planted a vineyard for Brookside Winery. Seizing a great opportunity, Ely Callaway jumped into the wine business. He planted 134 acres of premium grape varieties and built the first commercial winery in Temecula Valley.

Ely knew marketing from his previous experience as president of Burlington Industries, the world's largest textile firm. He promoted his wine prolifically and in 1976 his Riesling was chosen to be served to Queen Elizabeth and Prince Philip at the New York Waldorf-Astoria. The queen placed her vote on the Callaway Riesling when she asked for a second glass. Callaway wines were then the first Southern California wines to be placed on premium wine lists and in stores across the country.

Callaway infiltrated Southern California with a sales team of attractive and intelligent young women who enjoyed a good success persuading local restaurants and stores to carry Callaway products. He also made his winery a destination for tastings, wine appreciation classes, barbecues, and dinners.

With the success and name recognition that Ely Callaway brought to Temecula wines, it was a given that other successes would follow. Within a few years more vineyards were planted and wineries opened their doors: Hart Winery, Baily, Cilurzo, Maurice Car'rie, Mount Palomar Winery, Piconi, Mesa Verde Vineyards, Filsinger, and Glenoak Hills Winery. Then other wineries started: Bell, Falkner, Britton Cellars, Temecula Crest, Clos du Muriel, Culbertson, Van Roekel, Churon, Keyways, and more.

It was time to designate the Temecula Valley's viticulture area as a federally recognized wine region, to define the perimeters and to name it. A federally recognized region is called an "appellation".

After much discussion the Temecula Valley received formal recognition as an American Viticulture Area in 1984 as "Temecula AVA" and changed in 2004 to "Temecula Valley AVA". The area of designation follows the geographic outline of the Vail Ranch's onetime 87,500-acre holdings.

With a united appellation, whenever one winery was recognized, it accelerated everyone's success and brought more visitors into the Temecula Wine Country.

During the defining time between the planting of Temecula vineyards and the universal recognition of the outstanding flavor of the region's wines, there was a blind taste test in Paris in 1976 that changed the game for all California winemakers. Several esteemed French wine judges were given selected red and white wines to compare and to rate each wine numerically for their attributes. It was a huge surprise when all of the California wines were judged superior to the French wines for the first time in an international wine contest. This landmark competition is referred to as the 1976 Judgment of Paris and is recognized as a turning point in the appreciation of California wines.

A change came to the Temecula Valley when the television show *60 Minutes* broadcasted a report in 1991 called, *The French Paradox*. The question was why the French who drank red wine had less heart disease than their American counterparts who drank white wines. The answer was that resveratrol in red wines prevents damage to blood vessels, reduces cholesterol, and prevents blood clots. It was also mentioned that antioxidants in red wines help protect against cancer.

The *French Paradox* not only absolved the last vestige of guilt remaining from Prohibition, it gave permission and encouraged consumption of red wine.

More wineries opened and in 1988 John and Martha Culbertson offered the first fine dining in their Café Champagne where Martha prepared the menu and supervised preparation. The Culbertsons also offered the only sparkling wine in the valley made in the méthode champenoise. Martha offered cooking classes, including some taught by her friend Julia Child, and started the first jazz concerts in the Temecula Wine Country.

Temecula wines were getting noticed and won awards and accolades. The Culbertsons were flown to Tokyo on Air Force One to participate in a presidential trade mission. Culbertson champagnes were served for two of President Reagan's state dinners in the White House in 1986 and it was named the official wine of the American Orient Express train.

By then our wine country was on the map as a legitimate wine producing area. To attract and accommodate tourists, more restaurants opened, and lodging options were available at The Inn at Churon and Loma Linda Bed and Breakfast. With added amenities of food and lodging, the word was out that Temecula was a great weekend destination.

The Balloon and Wine Festival started in 1983, bringing big name musical talent, food, wine tasting, and views of myriads of balloons aloft. The annual event was widely publicized and still brings thousands of visitors to Temecula each year. In fact, on any given morning, balloons float about our countryside.

People who saw Jack Lemmon, Christine Lahti and Dudley Moore in the 1996 movie *Weekend in the Country*, filmed in Temecula, wanted to come to experience the Temecula Wine Country for themselves.

Our wine country gives varied experiences as it offers many choices of wines. We have offerings from Briar Rose's Snow White cottage to BOTTAIA's ultramodern complex, from the rustic Foot Path to the polished Monte De Oro Winery and everything in between.

Add today's beautiful amenities with music, dining and lodging and it would make a man like Vignes proud.

Some of our wineries are still owned by the families who first planted the vineyards and others harvest what someone planted before them. All are part of our story and attract people from all over the world.

A few years ago, Sheldon Lytton of Avensole Winery said, "There are now over 40 licensed wineries and 70 growers that farm vineyards throughout the Temecula Valley. The wines produced from our appellation are winning awards in California, across the United States, and even in France itself. Those wines, together with Temecula's magnificent climate and beautiful vistas, attract visitors from all over the world."

Wine Enthusiast magazine reviews hundreds of wines each month and reports on wine consumers' lifestyles. With the fine wines now produced in the Temecula Wine Country and the many amenities for dining, music, lodging, and entertainment, it is no wonder that in 2019 *Wine Enthusiast* magazine named the area "One of the 10 Best Wine Destinations in the World". Today our Wine Country has something for everyone, from Jeep tours to horseback treks, tranquil settings to club vibes. Everyone wants to come to the Temecula Wine Country.

Today locals and tourists drink deeply of the peaceful scenery and hospitality offered in the Temecula Wine Country as they satisfy their palates with the exceptional wines produced from grapes watered from deep reservoirs below the perfect mixture of decomposed granite baked in the right amount of sun before cooling breezes come from the ocean in the evening through the Santa Margarita Gap.

Vineyards flourish in *Temecula*, which means in the First People's language "the place of sun and sand".

In 50 years we went from unplanted and unknown to being one of the Top Ten Wine Destinations in the world!

PELTZER WINERY
A DAY WITHOUT WINE IS LIKE...
JUST KIDDING,
I HAVE NO IDEA

AKASH WINERY

"WE HOPE YOU EXPERIENCE A TASTE OF OUR DREAM IN EVERY GLASS."
— The Patel Family, owners, Akash Winery

In 2010, following a life-long dream, Ray, Nalini, and their son Akash Patel purchased 20 acres in the heart of Temecula's Wine Country. Together, the Patel's have learned the science of viniculture and alongside winemaker Renato Sais, have created wines that are "both unique and familiar."

Many of their wines are produced from estate grown grapes. However, their "Dreamville Wines" are created from varieties grown on nearby family-run vineyards. This allows Akash to "experiment and explore" with other varieties. Akash describes these wines as "easy-drinking, thoroughly enjoyable and approachable with a little less oak."

Their tasting room, which opened to the public in 2019, is bright, airy and echoes with the sound of laughter and glasses toasting. Akash Winery offers guests a refreshing and distinct experience unlike any other in the region.

They produce 5,000 cases of wine a year and have already won multiple gold, silver, and bronze awards for their wines.

New to Akash is their brewery. They believe in dreams and say, "The sky is the limit."

PARLEZ-VOUS ROSÉ • PARLEZ-VOUS
AKASH WINERY
2018 ROSÉ WINE
PARLEZ-VOUS ROSÉ

EXIT

NEW YORK STEAK WITH RED WINE JUS

SERVES 4 | PREP TIME: 5 MINUTES | COOK TIME: 20 MINUTES

4 (8 TO 10 OZ) NEW YORK STEAKS

3 TBSP OLIVE OIL

SALT AND PEPPER TO TASTE

RED WINE JUS

¾ CUP AKASH PETITE SIRAH

½ CUP BEEF STOCK

3 TBSP BUTTER, COLD, CUT INTO SMALL PIECES

1 ½ TBSP DIJON MUSTARD

Heat the oil in a heavy-bottomed pan big enough to hold the steaks without crowding.

Season steaks with salt and pepper and sauté in the oil until seared and brown.

Cook until interior reads 130 to 135°F on an instant thermometer. Transfer to a platter and let the steaks rest while you make the jus.

To make the red wine jus, add wine to the cooking pan and cook on medium-high heat until reduced to ⅓ cup. Add beef stock and cook until reduced to ½ cup.

Lower heat and whisk in butter and mustard.

To serve, spoon sauce over the steaks.

Pair with Celery Root and Potato Mash, recipe on page 19.

WINE PAIRING: Akash Winery | Petite Sirah | This decadent Petite Sirah boasts notes of blackberry, anise, and hints of cinnamon on the palate. It is rich in body with a velvety mouth feel that has layers of pepper and hints of dark chocolate that follow with a smooth tannin structure.

CELERY ROOT AND POTATO MASH

SERVES 8 | PREP TIME: 10 MINUTES | COOK TIME: 25 MINUTES

2 CELERY ROOTS (ABOUT 1 ½ LB EACH), PEELED AND CUT INTO 1 INCH CUBES

3 LB BAKING POTATOES (RUSSETS)

1 TSP SALT

½ CUP CREAM

4 OZ BUTTER

1 TBSP HORSERADISH, GRATED FRESH OR PREPARED IN A JAR

CHOPPED CHIVES FOR GARNISH

Place the celery root and potatoes in a saucepan and cover with cold water. Add 1 tsp salt. Bring to a boil, reduce heat and simmer until tender, approximately 15 to 20 minutes.

Drain the vegetables and pass through a food mill or a ricer into a large mixing bowl.

Stir in the cream, butter and horseradish until the mixture is smooth. Season with salt and pepper . Garnish with chopped chives.

Pair with New York Steak with Red Wine Jus, recipe on page 16.

OYSTERS CASINO

MAKES 18 OYSTERS | PREP TIME: 25 MINUTES | COOK TIME: 20 MINUTES

1 ½ DZ FRESH OYSTERS

3 SLICES BACON, DICED AND COOKED HALF-DONE

4 GREEN ONIONS, FINELY CHOPPED

¼ CUP BELL PEPPER, FINELY CHOPPED

¼ CUP CELERY, FINELY CHOPPED

1 TSP FRESH LEMON JUICE

1 TSP WORCESTERSHIRE SAUCE

ROCK SALT FOR COOKING AND SERVING

Preheat oven to 400°F.

Open the oysters and place on a baking sheet lined with rock salt.

Cook the bacon until half-done and drain on paper towels.

In the bacon drippings, cook the green onion, bell pepper and celery until tender.

Stir the lemon juice and Worcestershire sauce into the vegetables. Spoon onion mixture on the oysters and sprinkle the bacon on top.

Bake at 400°F for 10 minutes.

To serve, line individual casseroles or small plates with more rock salt. This keeps the oysters from sliding around.

WINE PAIRING: Akash Winery | Parlez-Vous Rosé | Hints of watermelon, strawberry and floral aromas.

ALTÍSIMA
WINERY
2020
Zinfandel
CALIFORNIA

ALTISIMA WINERY

Altisima, located along the DePortola Trail, offers a touch and taste of Spain. With wines made from Mourvèdre, Tempranillo, Grenache, the winery focuses on the early days of California when Spanish dons ruled the countryside. A beautiful view of the countryside is seen in every direction on the winery's twenty acres. Eight families are partners in this venture with longtime Temecula winemaker Marshall Stuart working his magic with the grapes to create delectable wines. The restaurant Gaspar offers a menu with a Spanish twist in homage to the explorer Gaspar de Portola, for whom the De Portola Trail is named. This new winery opened November 2021 and produces 15,000 cases per year.

SHRIMP CHILAQUILES WITH PINE NUT CREMA

SERVES 6 | PREP TIME: 15 MINUTES | COOK TIME: 45 MINUTES

TORTILLA STRIPS

6 TORTILLAS CUT INTO STRIPS 1 INCH WIDE

3 TBSP VEGETABLE OIL

SHRIMP CHILAQUILES

12 LARGE SHRIMP, CLEANED AND DEVEINED

4 TBSP OLIVE OIL

2 JALAPEÑOS, SEEDED AND DICED

2 DRIED NEW MEXICAN CHILES, BROKEN INTO PIECES

½ CUP ONION, CHOPPED

2 CLOVES GARLIC, MINCED

½ TSP SALT

2 CUPS CHICKEN STOCK

2 TSP MEXICAN OREGANO

Continued on page 26

To make the tortilla strips, preheat oven to 400°F.

Toss tortilla strips with the vegetable oil and bake for 12 minutes or until lightly toasted. Set aside.

To make the shrimp chilaquiles, preheat oven to 375°F.

Heat 2 tbsp of olive oil in a sauté pan and sauté the chiles, onion, and garlic until soft. Add the stock, salt, oregano and tomatillos. Bring to a boil, reduce heat and simmer until tomatillos are soft. Puree.

In a sauté pan, heat the remaining 2 tbsp of olive oil and cook the shrimp for about 1 ½ minutes each side.

Add the sauce, pepper and tortillas to the shrimp and simmer until tortillas are softened, about 3 minutes more.

Transfer the shrimp chilaquiles to an oven proof dish and top with Oaxacan cheese. Bake at 375°F for 10 minutes or until cheese is melted.

Continued on page 26.

WINE PAIRING: Altisima Winery | Zinfandel | Rich and complex with anise aromas, loganberry flavors and soft tannins.

8 TOMATILLOS, HUSKED, RINSED AND CHOPPED

½ TSP BLACK PEPPER

1 CUP OAXACAN CHEESE, SHREDDED

PINE NUT CREMA

SLICED RADISHES OR POMEGRANATE SEEDS

PINE NUT CREMA

2 TBSP OIL

½ CUP ONION, CHOPPED

1 CLOVE GARLIC, CHOPPED

2 TBSP CREAM CHEESE

1 CUP SOUR CREAM

½ CUP CHICKEN OR VEGETABLE STOCK

1 CUP PINE NUTS, TOASTED

SALT TO TASTE

Serve with pine nut crema and sliced radishes.

To make the pine nut crema, add the oil to a sauté pan. Add onion and garlic and sauté until browned. Add the cream cheese, sour cream, stock and 2 tbsp of the toasted pine nuts. Bring to a boil. Reduce heat and simmer for one minute. Let cool and puree until smooth.

Stir in the rest of the pine nuts.

"THIS SPICY COMFORT DISH ACCOMPANIED BY THE PINE NUT CREMA CAN BE SERVED FOR BRUNCH OR LUNCH AND IS A DINNER DISH PERFECT FOR GUESTS."

ENSALADA DE NOCHEBUENA

SERVES 10 TO 12 | PREP TIME: 1 HOUR

- 8 SMALL COOKED BEETS, THINLY SLICED
- 4 ORANGES, PEELED AND SECTIONED
- 4 RED APPLES, CORED AND SLICED (NOT PEELED)
- 4 BANANAS, PEELED AND SLICED (DO THIS JUST BEFORE SERVING)
- 1 FRESH PINEAPPLE, PEELED, CORED AND CUT INTO 1 INCH PIECES
- 1 CUP PEANUTS, CHOPPED
- 1 POMEGRANATE, SEEDS REMOVED AND RESERVED
- 1 CUP JICAMA, JULIENNED
- ½ CUP SEEDLESS RED GRAPES
- ½ CUP SEEDLESS GREEN GRAPES
- 1 PINK GRAPEFRUIT, PEELED AND SECTIONED
- 1 HEAD ROMAINE LETTUCE, CUT INTO CHIFFONADE

Place the lettuce into the bottom of a large shallow bowl.

Arrange the beets and fruit in overlapping circles on top of the lettuce

Sprinkle peanuts in center of circle and pile pomegranate seeds on top.

WINE PAIRING: Altisima Winery | Coqueta | A dry rosé, crisp and refreshing with a bouquet of strawberry, rhubarb, cherry and pomegranate.

DRESSING

2 CUPS SOUR CREAM

½ CUP LEMON JUICE

6 TBSP SUGAR

1 TSP SALT

¼ TSP ALMOND EXTRACT

1 CUP POMEGRANATE SEEDS

2 TSP LEMON ZEST

To make the dressing, combine all ingredients except lemon zest. Sprinkle lemon zest over the top. Refrigerate.

"This is a spectacular buffet centerpiece, which represents a poinsettia and the dressing is unusual and delicious."

AVENSOLE
WINERY
2016 RIESLING

AVENSOLE WINERY

"DISCOVERY AND ADVENTURE MAKE LIFE MEANINGFUL"
— Avensole Winery

Knowing that great fruit produces great wines, Avensole Winery's vineyard estate has produced some of Temecula's finest grapes for more than four decades as their many awards show. Avensole wines are made in a New World California style with a focus on Zinfandel, which is used to craft some of their favorite proprietary blends.

When the Lytton Family first saw the Van Roekel winery in 2013, they fell in love with it. In 2014, they purchased the winery and renamed it Avensole from the Italian word "avventura" (adventure) and "sole" ("one of a kind"). The Lyttons decided to make Avensole the family's greatest adventure of all.

A visitor finds a trendy tasting room a few steps from the restaurant down a pleasant walkway with a lush fountain and flowers that seem cool even on a warm day.

They produce roughly 6,000 cases of wine a year.

PORK CHOPS BRAISED WITH SAGE AND TOMATOES

SERVES 6 | PREP TIME: 5 MINUTES | COOK TIME: 50 MINUTES

- 2 TBSP BUTTER
- 1 TBSP OLIVE OIL
- 6 PORK LOIN CHOPS, ½ INCH THICK
- FLOUR FOR DREDGING
- 8 FRESH SAGE LEAVES OR 4 WHOLE DRIED LEAVES
- ½ TSP SALT
- ½ TSP PEPPER
- 1 (15 OZ) CAN ITALIAN PLUM TOMATOES, CHOPPED UP WITH THEIR JUICE

Preheat oven to 350°F.

Put the butter and olive oil into a large sauté pan.

Dredge the chops in flour.

Add the sage to the butter-oil mixture then add the chops and brown on each side.

Add chopped tomatoes and juice. Add salt and pepper.

Cover the pan and place in the oven for 35 to 45 minutes or until an instant thermometer reads 155 to 165°F.

Serve the chops with the pan juices.

WINE PAIRING: Avensole Winery | Sangiovese | This wine is a blend of Sangiovese and Grenache aged in French oak barrels. It delivers red fruit flavors with nuances of vanilla and spice.

ROMAINE SALAD WITH ROASTED POBLANO DRESSING

SERVES 4 | PREP TIME: 10 MINUTES

1 HEAD ROMAINE LETTUCE, TRIMMED AND CUT LENGTHWISE INTO QUARTERS

½ CUP OLIVE OIL

2 TBSP FRESH LIME JUICE

2 TBSP POBLANO CHILE, ROASTED, PEELED, SEEDED AND DICED

2 TBSP HONEY

SALT AND PEPPER

1 RIPE AVOCADO, PEELED AND SLICED LENGTHWISE

¼ CUP QUESO FRESCO FOR GARNISH

In a blender or food processor, blend the olive oil, lime juice, chile and honey until smooth.

Put one romaine quarter on a plate and layer ¼ of the avocado slices on the romaine.

Spoon some of the dressing over the salad and sprinkle with queso fresco.

"This Caesar-like salad with a spicy dressing makes a nice lunch dish with a baguette or some tortilla chips."

WINE PAIRING: Avensole Winery | Gewürztraminer | Stone fruit flavors complemented by hints of lychee with spicy undertones and a round finish.

BAILY VINEYARD AND WINERY

PHIL CRAFTS HIS WINES TO PRODUCE AN "OLD WORLD STYLE."

When Carol and Phil Baily left the Los Angeles area in 1981 to move to "the country", they chose land in the Temecula Valley that had been part of the 87,500-acre Vail Ranch cattle grazing operation. The former ranch was undergoing transformation with 3,000 acres designated as a wine region.

Being avid wine enthusiasts and home wine makers, the Bailys planted their first acre of grapes on Mother's Day in 1982. In 1983, they expanded the vineyard to six acres and began taking courses in viticulture and enology at the University of California, Davis. In 1986, they built their first small winery on Pauba Road and opened it with only one wine, *Cabernet Sauvignon for sale.*

Today they have 25 acres of grapes, with one vineyard being an original planting from 1968. Baily Vineyard and Winery believes that making wines from the same vineyards for over twenty years assures a consistency that few wineries in the region can match. They specialize in the Bordeaux varieties of Cabernet Sauvignon, Merlot, Cabernet Franc, Malbec, Sauvignon Blanc, and Semillon. Phil crafts his wines to produce an "Old World Style" characterized by restrained alcohol and higher acidity, emphasizing elegance and finesse as opposed to boldness and power. To this end, the grapes are picked at moderate sugar levels and the wines undergo longer barrel aging than the normal industry practice to produce more complex, less fruit-forward aromas, and more integrated tannins. They produce 6,000 cases of wine a year.

BAILY
2017
Temecula Valley
Estate Bottled
Chardonnay

RILLETTES OF TWO SALMONS

MAKES 2 CUPS | PREP TIME: 60 MINUTES | COOK TIME: 10 MINUTES

- 1 LB CENTER-CUT SALMON FILETS, SKIN AND BONES REMOVED AND TRIMMED
- 2 TBSP BRANDY
- 8 TBSP BUTTER, AT ROOM TEMPERATURE
- ½ CUP MINCED SHALLOTS
- 1 TBSP CRÈME FRAÎCHE
- 8 OZ SMOKED SALMON, CUT INTO ¼ INCH DICE
- 2 ½ TBSP LEMON JUICE
- 1 TSP OLIVE OIL
- 2 LARGE EGG YOLKS, LIGHTLY BEATEN
- ½ CUP CLARIFIED BUTTER, COOLED TO ROOM TEMPERATURE
- SALT AND PEPPER
- FRESH CHIVES, MINCED, FOR GARNISH (OPTIONAL)

Place the salmon filets in a shallow dish and sprinkle each side with the brandy, 1 ½ tsp salt and ¼ tsp pepper. Cover and refrigerate for 1 hour, turning the fish over halfway through the marinating process.

Bring water to boil in the bottom of a steamer. Place the salmon in the steamer and cover. Steam gently for 8 minutes. Probe the salmon with a fork. The center should be medium rare. Remove the salmon filets and let cool.

Melt 1 tbsp butter in a medium sauté pan. Add the shallots and cook on medium heat until transparent.

Put the remaining 7 tbsp butter in a bowl and beat with a spatula until smooth. Stir in the crème fraîche and set aside.

Put the cooked salmon in a bowl and break it into large chunks. Stir in the smoked salmon, lemon juice, olive oil and egg yolks. Season with salt and pepper. Fold in the butter mixture.

Transfer the mixture into crocks leaving at least ½ inch space at the top. Smooth the top of the rillettes and refrigerate until cold.

Pour a ¼ inch thick layer of clarified butter over the top of the rillettes to seal. Cover and store in the refrigerator for up to a week.

To serve, remove the butter layer. Spread the rillettes on toasts and sprinkle with chives.

WINE PAIRING: Baily Vineyard and Winery | Chardonnay | This Chardonnay has a great balance of fruit and oak flavors.

AMARETTI TORTE

SERVES 8 TO 10 | PREP TIME: 20 MINUTES | COOK TIME: 45 MINUTES

10 AMARETTI COOKIES

1 CUP BUTTER, AT ROOM TEMPERATURE

1 CUP SUGAR

5 LARGE EGGS, SEPARATED

½ CUP ALL PURPOSE FLOUR

4 OZ SEMI-SWEET CHOCOLATE, GRATED

POWDERED SUGAR

Preheat oven to 350°F.

Butter and flour a 9 inch cake pan.

Put the cookies into a food processor and process until they become crumbs.

Cream the butter and sugar and beat in the 5 egg yolks, one at a time. Continue beating for 10 minutes. Gradually add the flour and amaretti cookie crumbs, beating after each addition. Fold in the chocolate.

Beat the egg whites in a seperate bowl until stiff and fold them into the batter. Pour the batter into the prepared cake pan.

Bake for 45 minutes or until a toothpick inserted in the middle of the cake comes out clean.

Let cool on a rack. Just before serving, sprinkle with powdered sugar.

NOTE: To acheive a beautiful powdered sugar design, start by laying a cake stencil of your choosing on top of the cake and sprinkle with powdered sugar. Then, carefully remove the stencil.

WINE PAIRING: Baily Vineyard and Winery | Serenity | Serenity is 68% Sauvignon Blanc and 32% Semillon, and at 7% residual sugar, is sweet but balanced by crisp acidity.

FILET OF BEEF WITH CABERNET SAUCE

SERVES 6 TO 8 | PREP TIME: 15 MINUTES | COOK TIME: 30 MINUTES

1 (2 ½ LB) BEEF TENDERLOIN

3 TBSP BUTTER

CABERNET SAUCE

1 TBSP BUTTER

½ CUP SHALLOTS, CHOPPED

1 TSP BLACK PEPPERCORNS, CRUSHED

2 THYME SPRIGS

2 CUPS BAILY CABERNET SAUVIGNON

½ CUP WHIPPING CREAM

1 TBSP PREPARED HORSERADISH

Preheat oven to 425°F.

Sprinkle the beef tenderloin with salt and pepper.

Melt the butter in a roasting pan over high heat. Sear the meat on all sides, 5 to 6 minutes.

Place in oven for 18 to 20 minutes. A meat thermometer should register approximately 135°F for medium rare. See chart below for additional doneness temperatures.

Doneness Temperature for Beef Roasts
Rare: 125°F | Medium Rare: 135°F
Medium: 145°F | Medium Well: 160°F

When the beef tenderloin has reached desired temperature, remove from oven and place the meat on a heated serving platter. Allow the meat to rest for 10 to 20 minutes.

While the tenderloin is roasting, make the cabernet sauce. Melt the butter in a heavy medium saucepan over medium heat. Add shallots, peppercorns and thyme. Sauté until shallots are tender, about 5 minutes. Add 2 cups cabernet sauvignon. Increase heat and boil until liquid is reduced to 1 cup, about 20 minutes. Strain sauce and return to same saucepan. Add ½ cup whipping cream and boil until reduced, about 7 minutes. Stir in horseradish. Season sauce to taste with salt and pepper.

To serve, plate beef and spoon sauce over top or serve with sauce on side.

Pair with Potato Gratin with Leeks and Fresh Thyme, recipe on page 43.

WINE PAIRING: Baily Vineyard and Winery | Cabernet Sauvignon | This wine offers warm, rich tones with subtle, herbaceous qualities and a hint of mint.

POTATO GRATIN WITH LEEKS AND FRESH THYME

SERVES 8 | PREP TIME: 10 MINUTES | COOK TIME: 45 MINUTES

- 2 TBSP OLIVE OIL
- 2 LEEKS, HALVED LENGTHWISE AND THINLY SLICED
- 1 TSP FRESH THYME, CHOPPED
- 1 ½ TSP SALT
- ¼ TSP BLACK PEPPER
- 1 ½ LB RED POTATOES (ABOUT 2 INCHES IN DIAMETER), CUT INTO ⅛ INCH ROUNDS
- 1 ½ CUPS CHICKEN BROTH, HEATED

Preheat oven to 400°F.

Put the olive oil into a sauté pan and add the leeks, thyme, salt and pepper. Cook until softened, about 6 minutes. Transfer to a bowl and add the potatoes and toss to combine. Transfer the potato mixture to the baking dish.

Bake until the potatoes are tender and the tops golden brown, about 40 minutes.

Pair with Filet of Beef with Cabernet Sauce, recipe on page 42.

MUSHROOM AND CHEESE QUESADILLAS WITH FRESH MANGO SALSA

MAKES 18 WEDGES | PREP TIME: 30 MINUTES | COOK TIME: 5 MINUTES

- 2 TBSP OLIVE OIL
- 12 WHITE BUTTON MUSHROOMS, SLICED
- 1 CLOVE GARLIC, MINCED
- 1 TSP FRESH ROSEMARY, MINCED
- 1 TBSP BALSAMIC VINEGAR
- 2 TBSP BUTTER, MELTED
- 6 LARGE FLOUR TORTILLAS
- 3 OZ GOAT CHEESE, CRUMBLED
- 9 OZ MONTEREY JACK CHEESE, GRATED
- SALT AND PEPPER

Place a flat griddle or a large skillet over medium-high heat and brush the pan with melted butter.

Combine the goat cheese, garlic, rosemary and balsamic vinegar. Spread the goat cheese mixture on one side of a tortilla and place clean side down on the griddle.

Immediately scatter ⅓ of the Monterey Jack cheese on top, leaving a ½-inch border around the edge of the tortilla.

Top with three of the sliced mushrooms and place a second tortilla on top. Brush the top with butter.

Cook until the cheese begins to melt and the bottom tortilla is lightly browned. Turn the quesadilla over and cook the other side until lightly browned.

Transfer to a baking sheet and keep warm in a low oven. Repeat with the rest of the tortillas.

Transfer to a cutting board and cut each quesadilla into six wedges.

Serve with fresh mango salsa, recipe on page 45.

WINE PAIRING: Baily Vineyard and Winery | Rosé of Sangiovese | This Rosé of Sangiovese is fun, fruity and full of character. It is great at holiday meals, your guests will be delighted, and it will look amazing on your table next to the cranberry sauce!

FRESH MANGO SALSA

1 CUP FRESH MANGO, FINELY DICED

¼ CUP CUCUMBER, PEELED, SEEDED AND DICED

1 GREEN ONION, FINELY CHOPPED

1 TBSP FRESH LIME JUICE

¼ TSP SALT

BLACK PEPPER

To make the fresh mango salsa, combine all ingredients in a bowl.

Butterfly Effect
DRY RED WINE • CALIFORNIA
ALCOHOL 14.1% BY VOLUME
NET CONTENTS 750 ml

BEL VINO

ONE SIMPLE ACT OF KINDNESS CAN PRODUCE AN ENORMOUSLY POSITIVE EFFECT.

Ascending the driveway to Bel Vino, there is no indication of the marvelous view at the top. No other location in the Temecula Wine Country offers the commanding vista of nearly 360 degrees as the Bel Vino hilltop overlooking verdant vineyards.

The view isn't the only treat offered at Bel Vino. Because they believe in making great, award-winning wines, they use classic Old World techniques, making small batch, handcrafted wines. Each step in the process is tailored to the specific wine varietal, and each red wine is aged in oak barrels for a smooth finish. Their techniques take no shortcuts and do not compromise on quality.

Bel Vino has been in business since 1996, originally known as Stuart Cellars. The initial planting in the 1990s was done in rows running north to south in a time proven French tradition so the fruit is shaded by the vines during the heat of the day.

In 2011, with visionary new ownership, Bel Vino has become a popular destination for wine lovers and enthusiasts. They offer thirty to forty great wines, including their highly rated reds and several other gold medal winners. One of their favorite wines is their Butterfly Effect, a dry red blend of Cabernet Sauvignon, Merlot, and Cabernet Franc. It was created at Bel Vino's boutique winery and aged in oak barrels for 22 months, making it a smooth, flavorful, and aromatic wine. Named Butterfly Effect, it is to remind the taster how one simple act of kindness can produce an enormously positive effect.

Bel Vino produces about 10,000 cases of wine each year.

SPAGHETTI CARBONARA

SERVES 4 | PREP TIME: 5 MINUTES | COOK TIME: 15 MINUTES

1 LB DRIED SPAGHETTI

3 TBSP OLIVE OIL

1 GARLIC CLOVE

4 OZ PANCETTA, CUT INTO ¼ INCH DICE

2 EGGS

1 CUP PARMESAN, FRESHLY GRATED

Bring a large pan of water to a boil and add salt. Add the spaghetti and cook until al dente.

Beat the eggs in a bowl and mix in the cheese, set aside.

Heat the oil in a large frying pan over medium heat. Add the garlic and fry until golden. Discard garlic, leaving the oil in the pan. Add the pancetta. Sauté until lightly browned.

Before draining the spaghetti, reserve ½ cup of the pasta water. Drain spaghetti and add to the pan with pancetta. Add the pasta water and cook for 1 to 2 minutes to heat through.

Take the pan off the heat and stir in the eggs and cheese.

Serve immediately.

"Every cook needs a delicious, quick, go-to pasta in their repertoire. This is it for me."

WINE PAIRING: Bel Vino | Butterfly Effect | This is a dry red wine aged in oak which produces aromas of chocolate and cherry and flavors of jam, toasted oak, spices, vanilla and mocha.

ALTERNATIVE WINE PAIRING: Bel Vino | Merlot | Dry with deep fruit flavors of blackberry, blueberry and plum with strong chocolate notes and spices.

BAKED LEMON THYME CHICKEN

SERVES 6 | PREP TIME: 10 MINUTES | COOK TIME: 55 MINUTES

- 6 (5 OZ) CHICKEN BREASTS
- 1 TSP KOSHER SALT
- ¼ TSP BLACK PEPPER
- FLOUR FOR DREDGING
- 3 TBSP OLIVE OIL
- 3 CUPS ONIONS, THINLY SLICED
- 1 ½ TSP GARLIC, THINLY SLICED
- 1 ½ CUP CHICKEN STOCK, HEATED
- 2 LEMONS
- 8 FRESH THYME SPRIGS

Preheat oven to 400°F.

Season chicken with salt and pepper. Dredge chicken in flour. Heat 2 tbsp of oil in a pan and sear chicken pieces to a rich golden brown. Transfer the chicken to a plate and reserve.

Heat remaining oil in the pan and sauté the onions and garlic on medium heat until golden brown, about 15 minutes.

Spread the onion mixture over the bottom of the pan, or seperate baking dish, and lay thyme sprigs on top.

Arrange the browned chicken over onion mixture and add chicken stock.

Cut lemon into slices and place 1 slice atop each piece of chicken. Squeeze remaining lemon over chicken. Cover and place in oven.

After 15 minutes, remove cover, baste chicken and continue to cook uncovered for 20 to 25 minutes.

To serve, plate chicken with onion mixture spooned over.

WINE PAIRING: Bel Vino | Viognier | Dry, medium bodied wine with perfumed aromas of peach, tangerine and honeysuckle with creamy aromas of vanilla.

BOTTAIA
DOLCETTO
2014

BOTTAIA WINERY

THEIR NAMESAKE, BOTTAIA IS ITALIAN FOR "CASK-AGING ROOM."

The Ponte family started farming the historic Brookside Ranch north of Temecula in 1985 and decided to do something different. They replanted with Italian varieties ranging from Arneis to Zibibbo and have been delighted with the results. Their namesake, Bottaia is Italian for "cask-aging room" and embodies their winemaking philosophy beautifully.

Bottaia Winery crafts the Italian varietals using sustainable viticulture practices and modern winemaking applications informed by Old World traditions. Their red wines are first fermented in concrete tanks or oak vats, then aged in large capacity oak casks for a minimum of two years. They produce over a dozen single-varietal Italian wines and blends, all sourced from their estate vineyards in the Temecula Wine Country. Some of their white wines are fermented in concrete to give minerality and to balance the natural acidity of late ripening Italian white varieties.

Fermenting in oak or concrete vessels allows the flavors and aromas to develop differently than in stainless steel tanks. In addition, careful monitoring of temperatures during fermentation preserves the flavors and aroma of each variety. Bottaia Winery produces 10,000 cases of wine a year.

Bottaia Winery offers visitors the unique experience of blending wines in a wine lab setting to satisfy their personal palates and also offers a luxurious swimming pool and cabanas for enjoyment.

ROASTED BUTTERNUT SQUASH AND APPLE SOUP

SERVES 6 TO 8 | PREP TIME: 10 MINUTES | COOK TIME: 50 MINUTES

2 ½ LB BUTTERNUT SQUASH, PEELED, SEEDED AND CUT INTO 2 INCH PIECES

2 MEDIUM ONIONS, PEELED AND QUARTERED

3 CLOVES GARLIC, PEELED

2 APPLES SUCH AS GRANNY SMITH, PEELED, CORED AND QUARTERED

2 TBSP OLIVE OIL

4 CUPS CHICKEN STOCK

SALT AND PEPPER

APPLE CHIPS

2 CUPS WATER

1 ½ CUPS SUGAR

2 LEMONS, JUICED

2 SMALL APPLES

Preheat oven to 400°F.

In a large roasting pan, toss squash, onions, garlic and apples with the oil. Season with the salt and pepper. Roast, stirring every 10 minutes until vegetables are fork-tender and lightly browned, about 40 minutes.

Transfer half the vegetables and 2 cups of stock to a food processor and puree until smooth.

Repeat with remaining vegetables and broth. Return pureed mixture to pot thinning soup with more stock if necessary. Bring to a simmer.

Serve garnished with apple chips or bits of sautéed apple.

To make the Apple Chips, combine the water and sugar and bring to a gentle boil over medium heat. Cool.

Using a mandoline or sharp knife, cut each apple, placing the core end of the apple in front of the blade, into rounds as thin as you can manage. Remove any seeds as you cut. Sprinkle the apple slices with lemon juice and submerge them in the syrup and allow them to marinate overnight.

Preheat oven to 200°F.

Remove apples from the syrup and dry them on a kitchen towel. Place them on a baking sheet lined with parchment or on a tray fitted with a baking rack.

Bake until crispy, about 1 hour.

WINE PAIRING: Bottaia Winery | Dolcetto | A rustic wine with elegant fig and licorice aromas.

WILD MUSHROOM STUFFED TURKEY BREAST

SERVES 10 | PREP TIME: 25 MINUTES | COOK TIME: 45 MINUTES

8 TBSP BUTTER

4 OZ PANCETTA, CHOPPED

1 LEEK, CLEANED AND SLICED

1 RIB CELERY, DICED

2 CUPS WILD MUSHROOMS (SHITAKI, CREMINI, CHANTERELLES, ETC. OR A MIXTURE), SLICED

2 TSP HERBS DE PROVENCE

2 TBSP SHALLOTS, CHOPPED

1 CUPS CHICKEN STOCK (LOW SODIUM)

SALT AND PEPPER

2 CUPS FRESH BREAD CRUMBS

½ (2 TO 2 ½ LB) TURKEY BREAST, BONELESS AND BUTTERFLIED

Preheat oven to 375°F.

Heat a large sauté pan and sauté pancetta until lightly browned. Add 2 tbsp of butter, leeks and celery and sauté until soft. Add mushrooms and cook until they are tender, about 5 minutes. Add the herbs and shallots and cook for 2 more minutes. Add the stock, bring to a simmer. Season to taste with salt and pepper.

Place bread crumbs in a mixing bowl and pour the mushroom mixture over the bread crumbs. Mix well and cool.

Butterfly the turkey breast with a sharp flat knife. Using a meat mallet, pound the turkey breast between two sheets of plastic wrap until it is an even thickness. Salt and pepper inside. Spoon the stuffing lengthwise across the breast and roll up. Tie the stuffed turkey with twine. Season the outside with salt and pepper.

Melt 4 tbsp of butter and reserve for basting the turkey.

Add 2 tbsp of butter to the pan and brown all sides of the turkey. Put the pan in the oven, basting with the reserved melted butter every 15 minutes. Roast for 30 to 35 minutes or until a thermometer reaches 155°F. Remove from the oven, cover with foil and allow to rest 10 minutes before slicing.

WINE PAIRING: Bottaia Winery | Arneis | This elegant white wine has subtle fruit tastes.

Taste the Enchantment
Briar Rose
WINERY
Tempranill
Linkogle Estate Collection
TEMECULA VALLEY
Vintage 2012
Limited Production

BRIAR ROSE WINERY

"TASTE THE ENCHANTMENT"
— Les and Dorian Linkogle

Whether a visit to Briar Rose Winery or a taste of their award-winning wines, it is an indulgence for the senses. Les Linkogle purchased their charming winery property in the 1980s as a gift to his wife Dorian. Their grounds feature a life-size replica of the Grimm's Brothers Snow White's Cottage designed by Beldon Fields, a Disneyland designer. Following a dream, they planted a vineyard in 1995 and opened the Briar Rose Winery in 2007 where they offer first-class estate wines in the fairytale setting.

Briar Rose wines have been served everywhere from the White House to the Playboy mansion, and have won numerous international gold, silver, and bronze medals. Les has a passion for making premium wines beginning in the vineyard with a goal to harvest healthy, ripe grapes. The grapes are handpicked before crushing and only the finest grapes are selected to make into the 2,400 cases of wine Les makes each year.

Their signature reds include Cabernet Sauvignon and Zinfandel. Their whites include Viognier, Gewürztraminer and Riesling. Les makes some innovative and fun wines like Citronier, which is a blend of Viognier with Meyer lemon zest, and a wine lager Talking Frog, a blend of Viognier and lager Hefeweizen.

CHOUCROUTE GARNI

SERVES 10 | PREP TIME: 24 HOURS + 20 MINUTES | COOK TIME: 2 HOURS

DRY RUB

⅓ CUP KOSHER SALT

2 TBSP BROWN SUGAR

3 LB PORK BABY BACK RIBS, CUT INTO 3 SECTIONS

To make the dry rub, combine the salt and sugar.

Add the dry rub and pork ribs to a large resealable plastic bag. Shake well to coat the ribs with the seasonings. Refrigerate overnight.

WINE PAIRING: Briar Rose Winery | Viognier | Dry, medium bodied, perfumed aromas of peach, tangerine and honeysuckle with creamy aromas of vanilla.

20 JUNIPER BERRIES

15 BLACK PEPPERCORNS

½ TSP CARAWAY SEEDS

3 BAY LEAVES

1 TSP BLACK PEPPER

¼ CUP OLIVE OIL

1 LARGE ONION, THINLY SLICED

4 LARGE GARLIC CLOVES, COARSELY CHOPPED

1 (2 LB) PIECE BOILED HAM, SLICED ¼ INCH THICK

6 LB SAUERKRAUT FROM THE DELI SECTION, RINSED AND DRAINED

3 CUPS RIESLING WINE

3 CUPS CHICKEN STOCK

2 LB POTATOES (SUCH AS SMALL YUKON GOLD OR RED POTATOES), PEELED

3 LB SMOKED SAUSAGES (SUCH AS BRATWURST, KIELBASA, OR KNACKWURST), SKINNED AND CUT INTO 2 INCH SECTIONS

SALT AND PEPPER

ASSORTED MUSTARDS

Preheat oven to 325°F.

Place a heavy casserole dish over medium-high heat. Add the olive oil and brown the onion and garlic, cooking until softened.

Stir in the sauerkraut, juniper berries, bay leaves, caraway seeds, black pepper, stock and wine and bring to a boil.

Rinse the pork ribs with cold water to remove excess dry rub and pat dry. Nestle the pork ribs in the sauerkraut and bring back to a boil. Cover tightly with a lid, place dish in oven and braise for 1 ½ hours.

Remove the pork ribs from the sauerkraut and cut down between the ribs. Nestle the cut ribs, sausages and ham in the sauerkraut. Cover and bake until the meats are hot, about 30 minutes.

Place the potatoes in a pot with cold salted water and bring to a boil. Reduce heat and cook until tender. Drain potatoes and keep warm.

To serve, mound the hot sauerkraut in the center of warmed dinner plates and tuck in servings of the ribs, sausages and ham.

Serve with the boiled potatoes and assorted mustards.

PAELLA

SERVES 6 TO 8 | PREP TIME: 10 MINUTES | COOK TIME: 50 MINUTES

- ¼ CUP OLIVE OIL
- 3 CLOVES GARLIC, CUT IN HALVES
- 1 MEDIUM ONION
- 3 MEDIUM TOMATOES, BLANCHED, PEELED OR CHOPPED
- 1 SWEET RED PEPPER, SEEDED AND SLICED
- 3 LB CHICKEN, CUT INTO SERVING PIECES
- 4 OZ CHORIZO CUT INTO 1 INCH PIECES
- 1 TSP PAPRIKA
- 2 CUPS RICE
- ½ TSP SAFFRON
- 4 CUPS CHICKEN STOCK
- 1 CUP FROZEN PEAS
- ½ LB SHRIMP, SHELLED AND DEVEINED
- 1 LB MUSSELS OR CLAMS

Heat the oil in a large deep sauté pan or paella pan. Add the garlic and cook for two minutes to flavor the oil. Remove the garlic and discard.

Salt and pepper the chicken and cook until golden brown and remove from pan. Brown the chorizo and remove from the pan. Add the onions and sauté until translucent. Add the tomatoes, red pepper and paprika. Spread the rice in the pan and cook for 2 to 3 minutes more. Add the saffron to the chicken stock and pour over the rice mixture. Bring to a boil.

Place the browned chicken and chorizo back into the pan. Cover, reduce heat to medium-low and cook for 15 minutes more. Add the shrimp and mussels. Cover and cook 5 more minutes. Add the peas, cover and cook for an additional 5 minutes .

Serve from the paella pan.

WINE PAIRING: Briar Rose Winery | Tempranillo | This wine is a true Rioja-style Tempranillo with smoky aromas and flavors of plum, tobacco, vanilla, leather and herbs.

POTATO SALAD WITH WARM SAUSAGE

SERVES 6 | PREP TIME: 10 MINUTES | COOK TIME: 35 MINUTES

- 1 LB MILD OR SPICY SAUSAGE (CAN BE PORK OR CHICKEN)
- 8 SMALL RED POTATOES, QUARTERED
- 1 TBSP LEMON JUICE, PLUS THE ZEST FROM ONE LEMON
- ⅓ CUP OLIVE OIL
- 2 TBSP WHOLE GRAIN MUSTARD
- 1 TBSP FRESH TARRAGON, MINCED
- 4 RIBS CELERY, CUT INTO ¼ INCH DICE
- ½ CUP RED ONION, DICED
- SALT AND PEPPER

Sauté the sausages until cooked through, or roast in a 450°F oven for 15 to 20 minutes. When cooked through, slice into ½ inch rounds and reserve.

Place the potatoes in a saucepan with cold water, add salt and bring to a boil. Boil for 10 minutes or until tender. Drain and let cool.

Whisk the lemon juice, oil, mustard, tarragon, pinch of salt and a generous sprinkling of pepper in a large bowl. Add the sausages, potatoes, celery, onion and lemon zest.

Toss together and serve at room temperature.

Pair with Market Salad with Warm Goat Cheese and Hazelnuts, recipe on page 68.

WINE PAIRING: Briar Rose Winery | Estate Briar Rosé | Fresh on the palate with crisp acidity and opens with ripe strawberry, kiwi and honeysuckle flavors finishing with herbal aromas and mineral tones.

MARKET SALAD WITH WARM GOAT CHEESE AND HAZELNUTS

SERVES 6 | PREP TIME: 15 MINUTES | COOK TIME: 20 MINUTES

½ CUP HAZELNUTS, SKINNED

6 (2 OZ) DISKS OF FRESH GOAT CHEESE

6 OZ BABY GREENS OR A MIXTURE INCLUDING ARUGULA

2 TBSP SHALLOTS, MINCED

2 TBSP CHIVES, MINCED

¼ CUP PARSLEY LEAVES

½ CUP TARRAGON LEAVES

SALT AND PEPPER

Preheat oven to 350°F.

Place the hazelnuts on a baking sheet and bake for 3 to 4 minutes, until lightly browned. Let cool. Cut half of the hazelnuts in half and reserve for the salad. Chop the remaining hazelnuts and set aside for the goat cheese croutons.

Place one disk of goat cheese on each crouton and top with 2 tsp of the chopped hazelnuts. Place in the oven to warm for about 5 minutes or until the cheese is soft enough to spread.

Place the greens in a mixing bowl and toss with the shallots, herbs, hazelnut halves and just enough dressing to coat the greens lightly. Season with salt and pepper.

Arrange a mound of the salad on each serving plate and place a goat cheese crouton at its side.

Pair with Potato Salad with Warm Sausage, recipe on page 67.

WINE PAIRING: Briar Rose Winery | Barbera | Barbera is a red Italian wine grape variety evening. A natural bouquet with a hint of berries and a slight peppery taste, which turns to an enhanced finish. It's dark red but the taste is light.

VINAIGRETTE

½ CUP DIJON MUSTARD

½ CUP RED WINE VINEGAR

1 ½ CUPS CANOLA OIL

To make the vinaigrette, combine the mustard and vinegar in a blender and blend for 15 seconds. With the machine running, drizzle in ½ cup of the canola oil. Transfer the dressing to a bowl and add the remaining oil in a slow stream, whisking constantly.

CROUTONS

1 BAGUETTE

OLIVE OIL FOR DRIZZLING

SALT

To make the croutons, preheat oven to 350°F.

Cut the baguette on diagonal to make slices that are about 4 inches long. You need 6 slices for the salad. Place the croutons on a baking sheet, drizzle both sides lightly with olive oil and sprinkle with a pinch of salt. Place in oven for 10 minutes, then turn to other side and continue baking for 10 more minutes.

SKIRT STEAK WITH CARAMELIZED SHALLOTS AND RED WINE JUS

SERVES 4 | PREP TIME: 10 MINUTES | COOK TIME: 20 MINUTES

1 ½ LB SKIRT STEAK, CUT INTO 4 PIECES

¼ CUP CANOLA OIL

4 TBSP BUTTER

4 CUPS SHALLOTS (ABOUT 6 LARGE SHALLOTS), THINLY SLICED

4 TSP FRESH THYME, FINELY MINCED

SALT AND PEPPER

1 CUP FULL-BODIED RED WINE (SUCH AS CABERNET SAUVIGNON)

2 ½ TBSP BUTTER

Preheat oven to 375°F.

Season steaks with salt and pepper.

Add 2 tsp of canola oil to two skillets. When the oil is hot, add 1 tbsp butter to each skillet.

Add the steaks and sear one side until browned, then sear the second side. Transfer the meat to a baking sheet.

Add half of the sliced shallots to each skillet and cook for 2 minutes, until they start to soften. Combine the shallots into one skillet and add the remaining 2 tbsp butter and the thyme. Cook until shallots are softened and golden brown.

Taste, and season with salt and pepper and cook for an additional 2 to 3 minutes.

Spread the shallots over the steaks.

Place in the oven for 5 minutes or until the steaks are medium.

Add the wine to the pan which held the steaks and scrape up the browned bits from the pan bottom. Cook until the wine has reduced by half. Whisk in the butter. Keep warm.

To serve, plate steaks and spoon over the red wine jus.

NOTE: For a more elevated red wine jus recipe, see next page.

WINE PAIRING: Briar Rose Winery | Cabernet Sauvignon | This wine has aromas of blueberry, cherry and tobacco with flavors of cherry, plum, mint and vanilla. It finishes with accents of chocolate.

RED WINE JUS

1 BOTTLE CABERNET SAUVIGNON

1 CUP ONION, DICED

1 CUP CARROTS, PEELED AND SLICED

1 CUP LEEKS, SLICED

1 CUP SHALLOTS, SLICED

1 CUP BUTTON MUSHROOMS, SLICED

3 FRESH THYME SPRIGS

6 ITALIAN PARSLEY SPRIGS

2 BAY LEAVES

½ TSP BLACK PEPPERCORNS

3 LARGE GARLIC CLOVES

5 CUPS CHICKEN STOCK

Combine all ingredients except stock and bring to a boil. Simmer for 45 minutes or until the wine has reduced almost to a glaze.

Add the stock and simmer for 30 minutes.

Prepare an ice bath. Strain the jus through a fine mesh strainer or a colander lined with cheesecloth.

Cool in the ice bath.

NOTE: Can be stored for three days or frozen.

CALLAWAY
VINEYARD & WINERY
"Where the sun shines through the mist"
Special Selection
SAUVIGNON BLANC
CALIFORNIA
2016

CALLAWAY VINEYARD AND WINERY

"WATER SEPARATES PEOPLE, BUT WINE BRINGS PEOPLE TOGETHER."
— John Moramarco, winemaker, Callaway Vineyard and Winery

Vincenzo Cilurzo may have planted the first commercial vineyard in the Temecula Valley, but Callaway opened the first winery – attracting attention that benefitted the entire Temecula Valley Wine Country. Together, marketing expert Ely Callaway and viticulturist John Moramarco, a fourth generation winemaker, put Temecula Valley on the map of notable vinification regions. In 1976, Callaway wines received special acclaim when Queen Elizabeth requested a second glassful after toasting with their White Riesling at the Waldorf Astoria.

The fruit for Callaway wines is primarily sourced from vineyards in the Temecula Valley region where the grapes benefit from the cool air from the Pacific Ocean and a long and mild growing season. Today, Callaway's extensive line of premium, fruit forward wines are highly acclaimed. Carefully crafted, Callaway wines are well balanced, with crisp character, perfectly complementing today's lighter, eclectic cuisine. Half a century later, Callaway's legacy continues, with the Callaway Vineyard and Winery producing 15,000 cases of wine a year.

DUCK WITH SAUSAGE AND LENTILS

SERVES 6 | PREP TIME: 30 MINUTES | COOK TIME: 55 MINUTES

3 LARGE DUCK BREASTS

SALT AND PEPPER

Continued on page 78

Preheat the oven to 400°F.

Score the fat of the duck breasts in a criss-cross pattern. Season the duck with salt and pepper

Warm a sauté pan and place the duck breasts, fat side down in the skillet to render the fat, about 6 minutes.

Reserve duck fat.

Turn the duck breasts over and sear for 1 minute. Turn the fat side down again and place the skillet in the oven to roast for 7 to 10 minutes. The duck breasts should be cooked medium rare to medium. Medium temperature on an instant thermometer is 140°F. Keep warm.

Continued on page 78.

WINE PAIRING: Callaway Vineyard and Winery | Profunde | A blend of Cabernet Sauvignon, Syrah and Petite Verdot this is a deep and intense fusion of jammy blackberry, ripe strawberry and black licorice.

LENTILS

2 CUPS GREEN OR BROWN LENTILS

4 ½ CUPS WATER

1 TSP SALT

1 ½ LB MILD ITALIAN SAUSAGE WITH FENNEL

2 TBSP OLIVE OIL

2 ONIONS, FINELY CHOPPED

2 CARROTS, FINELY CHOPPED

1 RIB CELERY, FINELY CHOPPED

2 TBSP GARLIC, CHOPPED

1 TBSP ROSEMARY, FINELY CHOPPED

1 CUP RED WINE

1 CUP STOCK, BEEF OR CHICKEN

GARNISH

½ CUP PANKO CRUMBS, SAUTÉED IN 2 TBSPS RESERVED DUCK FAT.

To make the Lentils, in a saucepan combine the lentils and the water and bring to a boil. Reduce the heat to low and add salt. Simmer until the lentils are tender but firm, 30 to 40 minutes. Check the doneness often and add hot water if needed.

Prick the sausages in a few spots. Add olive oil to a sauté pan and add the sausages. Cook until browned. Remove from the pan and set aside.

Add the onions, carrots and celery to the pan and sauté until softened, about 10 minutes. Add the garlic and rosemary and cook until the vegetables are tender.

In a large pot combine the lentils, sausages, vegetables, wine and stock and cook until the pan juices have thickened.

Sprinkle the bread crumbs over the lentils as you serve.

Slice the duck breasts and arrange over the lentils.

"ALL THE
INGREDIENTS IN
THIS RUSTIC DISH
COME TOGETHER
IN PERFECT
HARMONY."

WILD MUSHROOM RISOTTO

SERVES 6 | PREP TIME: 30 MINUTES | COOK TIME: 40 MINUTES

1 OZ DRIED MUSHROOMS

½ LB FRESH CREMINI MUSHROOMS, CLEANED AND SLICED

4 CUPS CHICKEN STOCK

6 TBSP BUTTER

2 OZ PANCETTA, DICED

½ CUP SHALLOTS (ABOUT 3 SHALLOTS), CHOPPED

1 ½ CUPS ARBORIO RICE

½ CUP WHITE WINE

½ TSP SAFFRON THREADS

1 TSP SALT

½ TSP BLACK PEPPER

⅔ CUP PARMESAN CHEESE (SOME EXTRA FOR GARNISH), GRATED

2 TBSP BUTTER

Place the dried mushrooms in a bowl and pour 2 cups boiling water over them. Set aside for 30 minutes.

Remove the mushrooms, reserving the liquid. Rinse the rehydrated mushrooms once more, and set aside.

Strain the mushroom liquid through a coffee filter or paper towel, carefully discarding the sandy residue. Reserve the liquid.

Combine the chicken stock with the reserved mushroom liquid in a saucepan and bring to a simmer.

In a heavy bottomed pot, melt the butter and sauté the pancetta and shallots for 5 minutes. Add the rehydrated and cremini mushrooms and sauté for another 5 minutes. Add the rice and stir to coat the grains.

Add the wine and cook for 2 minutes. Add 2 full ladles of the chicken stock mixture to the rice, plus the saffron, salt and pepper. Stir and simmer until the stock is absorbed. Continue to add the stock mixture, 2 ladles at a time. Cook until the mixture seems a little dry before adding more of the stock mixture.

Continue until the rice is cooked through, but still al dente, about 20 to 25 minutes total.

When done, the risotto should be creamy and not dry.

Take off the heat and stir in the Parmesan cheese and butter.

Serve with extra Parmesan if you like.

WINE PAIRING: Callaway Vineyard and Winery | Sauvignon Blanc | Crisp and clean aromas of white peach crunchy pear and honeydew melon. Finishes with refreshing lemon curd, citrus peel and kumquat.

STUFFED ZUCCHINI BLOSSOMS WITH HEIRLOOM TOMATO SALAD

SERVES 4 TO 8 | PREP TIME: 20 MINUTES | COOK TIME: 10 MINUTES

½ LB FRESH MOZZARELLA, CUBED

¼ CUP PARMESAN, GRATED

¼ CUP FRESH BASIL, CHIFFONADE

8 ZUCCHINI FLOWERS

4 HEIRLOOM TOMATOES, CUT INTO SMALL WEDGES

4 GREEN ONIONS, SLICED VERY THIN ON THE BIAS

RED WINE VINEGAR

OLIVE OIL

1 CUP FLOUR

½ CUP WHITE WINE

VEGETABLE OIL TO FRY

Toss together the mozzarella, Parmesan and 2 tbsp of the basil chiffonade. Gently stick your finger inside the blossom and break off the stamen.

Shape the cheese mixture into an oblong shape to stuff into the blossom.

Press the blossom against the cheese to close. Refrigerate until ready to fry.

Toss the tomatoes with the scallions and remaining basil. Sprinkle with salt and add a drizzle of red wine vinegar and olive oil. Taste for seasoning. Reserve.

Mix the flour and ½ cup of wine. Mix until it is a loose batter. Add more wine if needed.

Add vegetable oil to a saucepan to a depth of one inch. Heat the oil and test by dropping a couple of drops of the batter into it. When they float immediately the oil is ready.

Dip a blossom into the batter and carefully drop it into the oil. Fry on both sides until they are golden brown, about 3 to 4 minutes

Drain the blossoms on paper towels and sprinkle with salt.

To serve as an appetizer, put the tomato salad in the center of a plate and arrange the stuffed zucchini blossoms around the tomato salad.

WINE PAIRING: Callaway Vineyard and Winery | Chardonnay | A light, crisp Chardonnay that opens with aromas of pineapple, citrus, apple and tropical fruit.

CARTER ESTATE WINERY AND RESORT

"REMEMBER, GENTLEMEN, IT'S NOT JUST FRANCE WE ARE FIGHTING FOR, IT'S CHAMPAGNE." — Winston Churchill

The Carter Estate Winery and Resort calls themselves "Temecula Valley's Hidden Gem." The winery is surrounded by 109 acres of vines enriched by lush soil and warmed by bright sunshine. Their sparkling wines are a delight to the senses.

Their wines are made from grapes one hundred percent estate grown, bottled, and certified sustainable – meaning Carter Estate Winery and Resort has complete control over their growing, bottling, and winemaking practices. Carter Estate Winery and Resort only produces sparkling wine produced in the Méthode Champenoise. Strict guidelines dictate, "Champagne" can only be made in the Champagne region of France and only from grapes grown in that region. However, many sparkling wines are made outside the Champagne region in France. These fermented sparkling wines have been identified as Méthode Champenoise sparkling wines until recently, and are now referred to as Méthode Traditionnelle. Carter Estate has mastered the art of Méthode Champenoise or Méthode Traditionnelle and is the only Temecula winery to do so. Their sparkling wines win awards every year thanks to the expert knowledge and leadership of winemakers Jon McPherson and Javier Flores. Carter Estate produces 2,400 cases of Méthode Traditionnelle and 3,000 cases of table wine a year. Sipping one of their sparkling wines makes a person smile.

Carter Estate
Carter Estate
CHARDONNAY
PRIVATE RESERVE
SOUTH COAST
LOT NO.
0002
VINTAGE
2014

SINGAPORE NOODLE SOUP

SERVES 10 TO 12 | PREP TIME: 30 MINUTES | COOK TIME: 15 MINUTES

2 LB CHICKEN (YOU CAN USE DARK OR LIGHT–A ROASTED CHICKEN FROM THE MARKET WORKS VERY WELL), COOKED AND SHREDDED

6 CUPS CHICKEN STOCK, HOME MADE OR PACKAGED

¼ CUP SOY SAUCE

3 GARLIC CLOVES, PEELED AND MINCED

2 TBSP FRESH GINGER, PEELED AND MINCED

3 TBSP LIME JUICE, FRESHLY SQUEEZED

2 TBSP BROWN SUGAR

1 TSP RED PEPPER FLAKES (OPTIONAL)

¼ CUP WATER

½ LB CELLOPHANE OR GLASS NOODLES

1 SMALL RED ONION, HALVED AND SLICED

1 BUNCH GREEN ONIONS, THINLY SLICED

24 FRESH MINT LEAVES

24 FRESH CILANTRO LEAVES

2 CUPS FRESH BEAN SPROUTS

1 ENGLISH CUCUMBER, PEELED, HALVED AND THINLY SLICED LENGTHWISE

2 LIMES, CUT INTO WEDGES FOR SERVING

In a medium bowl, whisk together the soy sauce, garlic, ginger, lime juice, sugar, red pepper flakes and ¼ cup water. Cover and set aside.

Soak noodles in warm water for 15 minutes and drain well. Bring stock to a simmer and stir in the soy sauce mixture. Divide the noodles among individual soup bowls, arrange chicken and noodles on top, then add sliced red onion and green onions. Ladle the hot stock over the prepared soup bowls.

Serve immediately topped with the mint leaves, cilantro, bean sprouts, and cucumber. Accompany with the cut limes.

WINE PAIRING: Carter Estate Winery and Resort | Chardonnay | Aged in French oak, this wine has flavors of toasty oak with hints of vanilla and tropical aromas with a baked apple pie flavor.

BLUEBERRY GALETTE

MAKES 8 TO 10 SERVINGS | PREP TIME: 30 MINUTES | COOK TIME: 40 MINUTES

PASTRY CRUST (PÂTE SUCRÉE)

2 CUPS ALL PURPOSE FLOUR

6 OZ SWEET BUTTER, SOFTENED AND CUT INTO PIECES

½ CUP SUGAR

¼ TSP SALT

⅓ CUP ICE WATER

FILLING

1 ½ CUPS FRESH BLUEBERRIES

2 TBSP GRANULATED SUGAR

1 TBSP FRESH LEMON JUICE

TOPPING

½ CUP ALL PURPOSE FLOUR

⅓ CUP LIGHT BROWN SUGAR, FIRMLY PACKED

¼ CUP OLD FASHIONED ROLLED OATS

½ TSP CINNAMON

3 TBSP BUTTER, MELTED

Place all pastry crust ingredients, except water, into the bowl of a food processor. Pulse until the flour mixture is incorporated and resembles corn meal. While motor is running add ice water. Pulse until the dough collects into a ball in the machine. Pour out onto a floured surface and shape into a disk. Wrap in plastic and refrigerate for 30 minutes.

Preheat the oven to 375°F.

Roll the dough into a 12 inch round about ¼ inch thick (rolling it on parchment makes it easier to transfer to a baking sheet). Transfer the dough to a baking sheet.

For the filling, stir together the blueberries, granulated sugar and lemon juice. Spread the blueberry mixture over the dough, mounding it slightly toward the center, leaving a 2 inch border. Fold the sides of the galette up and over the filling leaving the center open.

For the topping, stir the flour, brown sugar, oats and cinnamon together. Add the melted butter and stir until the mixture is mixed together. Sprinkle the top of the galette with the topping.

Bake until the crust is golden and the fruit is bubbling, about 40 minutes. Transfer the baking sheet to a wire rack and let cool. Cut into wedges to serve.

WINE PAIRING: Carter Estate Winery and Resort | Day Break | This muscat wine is fortified with grape brandy and has flavors of woody muscat and caramel and aromas of orange peel, apricot and honeysuckle.

CHAPIN FAMILY VINEYARDS

WINES "FOR THE LOVE OF FRIENDSHIP." – The Chapin Family

Steve Chapin, a Southern California native, founded Chapin Family Vineyards, a small boutique winery in the Temecula Valley. In college, Steve focused on microbiology and zoology, but after a tour of duty in the Navy and some experience in the business world, he found he enjoyed drinking quality wines and decided to plant his own vineyard on his property in Temecula Wine Country. In 2002, after several trips to wine producing regions, Steve Chapin planted five acres of Syrah, Cabernet Sauvignon, and Petite Verdot, supplying excellent grapes to other wineries in the region. A few years later, Chapin Family Vineyards planted another parcel with Viognier, Aglianico, and Montepulciano, with these first releases being sold primarily to hotels and restaurants. In 2012, Chapin Family Vineyards opened their tasting room to the general public. They now offer about fifteen different wines and produce 3,700 cases of wine a year.

The Chapin family believes in making small lots of handcrafted wines that offer intense flavor with depth and balance that best represents the Temecula Valley Appellation. They believe that 80% of the quality of wine comes from the vineyard. To achieve the desired quality of wine, they utilize European farming methods to encourage full-bodied, ripe wine grapes.

Chapin wines are aged in American and French oak barrels to provide fruit forward wines that have full-bodied complexity and soft finishes. Every Chapin label shares their philosophy "For the Love of Friendship".

Chapin
Eclipse
2016 Red Wine
Alcohol 13.5% by Volume

CHORIZO VERDE TACOS

SERVES 8 | PREP TIME: 20 MINUTES + 24 HOUR MARINADE | COOK TIME: 20 MINUTES

CHORIZO

2 LB GROUND PORK

½ CUP CILANTRO, CHOPPED

1 CUP PARSLEY, CHOPPED

2 CLOVES GARLIC

1 CUP OLIVE OIL

1 TBSP MEXICAN OREGANO

2 JALAPEÑOS, SEEDS REMOVED, CHOPPED

2 PASILLA CHILES, SEEDS REMOVED, CHOPPED

2 TBSP APPLE CIDER VINEGAR

1 CUP FRESH SPINACH, CHOPPED

1 BAY LEAF

½ TSP CUMIN

1 TSP SUGAR

1 TSP BLACK PEPPER

1 TBSP SALT

1 CUP ONION, CHOPPED

Continued on page 93

Place the pork in a bowl. Put the remaining ingredients in a blender and purée until smooth. Pour over the pork. Knead the meat until the purée is fully incorporated. Let the marinade stand in refrigerator for up to one day.

Heat a sauté pan, add the meat mixture and cook through.

Continued on page 93.

WINE PAIRING: Chapin Family Vineyards | Eclipse | A blend of Cabernet Sauvignon and Syrah. Aged in French and American oak which provides flavors of vanilla, caramel, almond and spice with subtle fruit flavors of blueberry, blackberry and black cherry.

ADDITIONAL INGREDIENTS

2 CUPS YUKON POTATOES, DICED

2 TBSP OLIVE OIL

TORTILLAS

GARNISH

FRESH SALSA

QUESO FRESCO

AVOCADO, SMASHED OR DICED

In a separate pan, sauté potatoes in 2 tbsp olive oil until cooked through.

Mix the chorizo and potatoes and serve in warm tortillas.

Garnish with cheese, avocado, and salsa.

WALNUT AND ROSEMARY FRIED CHICKEN

SERVES 4 | PREP TIME: 5 MINUTES | COOK TIME: 20 MINUTES

- ¼ CUP LOW-FAT BUTTERMILK
- 2 TBSP DIJON MUSTARD
- 4 TO 6 OZ CHICKEN BREASTS, POUNDED THIN
- ⅓ CUP PANKO BREAD CRUMBS, OR HOMEMADE BREAD CRUMBS, TOASTED
- ⅓ CUP WALNUTS, FINELY CHOPPED
- 2 TBSP PARMESAN CHEESE, GRATED
- ¾ TSP FRESH ROSEMARY, MINCED
- ¼ TSP KOSHER SALT
- ¼ TSP BLACK PEPPER
- COOKING SPRAY

Preheat oven to 425°F.

Combine buttermilk and mustard in a shallow dish, stirring with a whisk. Add chicken to mixture, turning to coat.

Heat a small skillet. Add bread crumbs to pan, cook on medium to high heat until golden, about 3 minutes. Remove from pan and let cool.

In a bowl, combine the toasted bread crumbs, nuts, Parmesan, rosemary, salt and pepper. Remove chicken from the buttermilk mixture and dredge it in the bread crumb mixture, making sure to evenly coat the breasts.

Arrange a wire rack on a large baking sheet. Coat rack with cooking spray. Arrange chicken on rack and coat chicken with cooking spray. Bake for 15 minutes or until an instant thermometer reads 160 to 165°F.

Ratatouille (recipe on page 103) makes a delicious accompaniment to the Walnut and Rosemary Fried Chicken.

WINE PAIRING: Chapin Family Vineyards | Rosella Rosé | 100% Montepulciano grapes. Delicate flavor with a hint of grapefruit and a slightly dry and crisp finish.

COUGAR VINEYARD AND WINERY

"A DAY WITHOUT WINE IS LIKE A DAY WITHOUT SUNSHINE."
— Rick and Jennifer Buffington, owners and winemakers, Cougar Vineyard and Winery

Rick and Jennifer Buffington started making wine over twenty years ago in Texas and later in Washington State. In 2005, when Rick and Jennifer purchased their property in Temecula, they found the area was especially suitable for Italian varietals. They planted Sangiovese, Aglianico, Montepulciano, Vermentino, Falanghina, Canaiolo Nero, Ciliegiolo, Glera, Piedirosso, Primitivo, Arneis, Malvasia Bianca, Pinot Grigio, Sagrantino, Nero d'Avola, Piedirosso and Lambrusca di Alessandria.

In 2006, Rick and Jennifer opened their family-owned boutique Cougar Vineyard and Winery. Cougar Vineyard and Winery produces exceptional Italian red, white and sparkling wines, as well as refreshing peach and strawberry sangrias in house with mostly estate-grown grapes. They also sell olives and olive oil pressed from their own olive trees. Cougar Vineyard and Winery produces 8,500 cases of wine annually and continues to increase production each year.

Aside from making excellent quality wines, the Buffingtons have made a huge contribution to the wine industry in America—notably their efforts in petitioning the Alcohol and Tobacco Tax and Trade Bureau (TTB) to recognize four varietals for sale in the US: Coda di Volpe, Falanghina, Brachetto, and Lambrusca.

The Buffingtons love the Temecula area for the sunshine and for the wine they make from grapes that ripen under the bright skies.

Cougar
VINEYARD & WINERY
LAMBRUSCA
di ALESSANDRIA
2015
Temecula Valley

CHOCOLATE ALMOND TORTE WITH CHERRY SAUCE

SERVES 8 TO 10 | PREP TIME: 15 MINUTES | COOK TIME: 30 MINUTES

CAKE

¼ CUP RAISINS

¼ CUP HOT COFFEE

10 OZ SEMI SWEET CHOCOLATE

6 OZ BUTTER

4 LARGE EGGS, SEPARATED

⅔ CUP SUGAR

⅔ CUP BLANCHED ALMONDS, GROUND INTO FLOUR

4 TBSP CAKE FLOUR

1 TSP VANILLA

CHERRY SAUCE

2 CUPS CHERRIES, FROZEN OR FRESH

⅓ CUP CHERRY JUICE

¼ CUP SUGAR

1 TBSP ARROWROOT

2 TBSP BRANDY

Preheat oven to 375°F.

Butter and flour a 9 inch spring form pan (can also use a 9 inch cake pan).

Pour the hot coffee over the raisins and let plump about 10 to 15 minutes.

Melt the chocolate over a bain-marie (double boiler) and beat together with the butter.

Separate the eggs. Beat the yolks and the sugar together. Add the raisins and coffee to the egg mixture then stir in the ground almonds, cake flour, vanilla and chocolate mixture.

Beat the egg whites until they hold stiff peaks. Stir in ⅓ of the egg whites into the batter to lighten and then fold in the rest of the beaten egg whites.

Bake 20 to 25 minutes until set.

Cool and unmold. Serve with cherry sauce.

To make the cherry sauce, in a small bowl, mix the arrowroot and brandy.

Combine the cherries, cherry juice and sugar in a saucepan and bring to a boil. Add the brandy and arrowroot mixture, reduce heat and simmer until the cherries soften slightly, 1 to 2 minutes.

"This recipe has been in my repertoire for at least forty years. I just recently added the cherry sauce. Cherries and chocolate....heaven."

WINE PAIRING: Cougar Vineyard and Winery | Estate Lambrusca di Allessandria | A bold and inky wine with aromas of black cherries and anise with a smooth finish.

QUESO FUNDIDO WITH GOAT CHEESE

SERVES 4 | PREP TIME: 10 MINUTES | COOK TIME: 15 MINUTES

- 2 TBSP OLIVE OIL
- ¼ CUP ONION, DICED
- 2 CLOVES GARLIC, PEELED AND THINLY SLICED
- 1 JALAPEÑO, SEEDS AND MEMBRANE REMOVED, CHOPPED
- ½ CUP TOMATO, DICED
- ½ CUP TOMATILLOS, DICED
- ¼ TSP SALT
- ¼ TSP PEPPER
- 8 OZ GOAT CHEESE
- TOASTED PUMPKIN SEEDS FOR GARNISH
- TORTILLA CHIPS

Sauté the onion, garlic and jalapeño in the olive oil until lightly browned. Add the tomato, tomatillo, salt and pepper and simmer until slightly thickened.

Turn on oven broiler.

Divide the cheese into 4 portions and place one piece in each of four ramekins. Top with the sauce. Place ramekins under the broiler until browned on top and heated through. Garnish with pumpkin seeds and serve with tortilla chips.

"A hearty appetizer which pairs well with the lusty and rustic Negroamaro."

WINE PAIRING: Cougar Vineyard and Winery | Estate Negroamaro | Rich with spicy notes of red fruit, coffee and blackberry.

RATATOUILLE

SERVES 8 TO 10 | PREP TIME: 15 MINUTES | COOK TIME: 45 MINUTES

- ⅓ CUP OLIVE OIL
- 2 GARLIC CLOVES, MINCED
- 1 LARGE ONION, SLICED
- 2 MEDIUM ZUCCHINI, CUT INTO 1 INCH CUBES
- 1 SMALL EGGPLANT, PEELED AND CUT INTO 1 INCH CUBES
- 3 TBSP FLOUR
- 1 (15 OZ) CAN OF PLUM TOMATOES, CHOPPED AND DRAINED
- 1 TBSP CAPERS, DRAINED
- SALT AND PEPPER

Heat the oil in a large skillet, add the garlic and onions and sauté until the onions are transparent.

Put the zucchini and eggplant into a bowl and toss with the flour.

Add the zucchini and eggplant to the skillet, cover and cook slowly for about 30 minutes.

Add the tomatoes and capers and simmer, uncovered for about 10 minutes.

Season with salt and pepper.

NOTE: This is delicious placed in a gratin dish, sprinkled with Parmesan and run under the broiler until the cheese is melted.

Pair with Walnut and Rosemary Fried Chicken, recipe on page 94.

SHRIMP MANICOTTI IN BECHAMEL SAUCE

SERVES 4 TO 6 | PREP TIME: 10 MINUTES | COOK TIME: 35 MINUTES

- 12 MANICOTTI OR CANNELLONI PASTA SHELLS
- 1 CUP RICOTTA CHEESE (WHOLE MILK)
- 1 CUP PARMESAN CHEESE, GRATED
- 1 LARGE EGG YOLK
- ½ CUP FRESH BASIL, CHOPPED
- 1 LB SHRIMP, CLEANED, DEVEINED AND CHOPPED
- ¼ TSP SALT
- ¼ TSP PEPPER
- BECHAMEL SAUCE

Preheat oven to 350°F.

Bring a pot of salted water to a boil and add the shells. Cook until al dente, about 10 minutes. Drain.

Mix together ricotta, ¾ cup Parmesan, egg yolk, basil, shrimp, salt and pepper.

Fill the cooked pasta shells with the shrimp mixture and place in a buttered baking dish.

Top the pasta shells with the béchamel sauce and sprinkle with ¼ cup Parmesan cheese. Bake until golden brown and bubbly.

To make the Bechamel Sauce, melt the butter in a saucepan and stir in the flour, whisking until smooth. Gradually add the warm milk whisking constantly until the sauce is thick and smooth. Add the salt, pepper and nutmeg.

BECHAMEL SAUCE

- 6 TBSP BUTTER
- 6 TBSP ALL PURPOSE FLOUR
- 4 CUPS WHOLE MILK, WARMED
- ½ TSP SALT
- ¼ TSP PEPPER
- PINCH FRESHLY GRATED NUTMEG

WINE PAIRING: Cougar Vineyard and Winery | Estate Coda di Volpe | A crisp light acidic white wine which has flavors of melon.

"THIS CAN BE MADE
THE DAY BEFORE
AND BAKED NEXT
DAY MAKING IT
A GREAT PARTY DISH."

DANZA DEL SOL WINERY

"WE ARE DEEPLY ROOTED IN TEMECULA VALLEY'S WINE HISTORY."
— Danza del Sol Winery

The Temecula vineyards that are now Danza del Sol Winery were originally planted with Zinfandel and Sauvignon Blanc in 1972. In 1978, Dr. William Filsinger, an Orange County pediatrician, purchased the 40-acre vineyard in Temecula. In 1980, William opened Filsinger Vineyard & Winery, honoring his family's legacy and providing closure to the sad memory of the Filsinger family vineyard in Mainz, Germany that was confiscated by the Nazis in WWII.

Filsinger planted more varietals, including Chardonnay, Cabernet, Gewürztraminer, Merlot and Viognier. The Filsingers were the first to grow Gewürztraminer grapes in Temecula, a variety that usually grows better in cooler climates. The Gewürztraminer wines won medals and became their most popular wine.

In 2010, following a successful career in the software business and rally car racing, Robert Olson purchased the Filsinger Vineyard & Winery. Olson brought new life to the winery, renaming the winery Danza del Sol, Italian for "Dance in the Sun" and adding varietals like Cabernet Franc, Tempranillo, Sangiovese, Syrah, Orange Muscat, Cabernet Sauvignon and Sauvignon Blanc.

Today, Danza del Sol Winery produces about 15,000 cases of wine a year. The friendly staff at Danza del Sol Winery prides themselves in producing affordable, quality, Mediterranean style wines to share with friends and family.

Danza del Sol
WINERY
PETITE SIRAH
2015 | TEMECULA VALLEY

BUTTERNUT SQUASH SOUP WITH WINE POACHED PEARS AND A BLEU CHEESE QUENELLE

SERVES 8 TO 10 | PREP TIME: 40 MINUTES | COOK TIME: 45 MINUTES

5 FRESH THYME SPRIGS

14 FRESH SAGE LEAVES

1 TBSP + ¼ CUP OLIVE OIL

1 MEDIUM ONION, DICED

1 CELERY STALK, DICED

1 CARROT, PEELED AND DICED

1 TSP GARLIC, MINCED

2 LB BUTTERNUT SQUASH, PEELED AND DICED

3 CUPS CHICKEN STOCK

Continued on page 111

In a large pot, add the 1 tbsp of olive oil and heat. Add the onion, carrot, celery and garlic and cook for 5 minutes. Add the butternut squash, broth and herb bundles (see note). Cook until the squash is soft, about 30 minutes. If using pre-cooked frozen squash, reduce cooking time to 15 minutes.

Remove herb bundles and ladle the soup into a blender, blend until smooth.

Add the ¼ cup oil to a sauté pan and heat. Add the remaining 10 sage leaves and cook until dark green and crispy, about 30 to 45 seconds. Drain on a paper towel.

Take one or two slices of the wine poached pears and put them in the bottom of a soup bowl. Pour the soup over the pears. Add a bleu cheese quenelle and top with a fried sage leaf.

NOTE: To make the herb bundles, bundle and tie the 5 fresh thyme sprigs and 4 fresh sage leaves with cooking twine.

Continued on page 111.

WINE PAIRING: Danza del Sol Winery | Gewürztraminer | Aromas of citrus blossoms and honey. Subtle sweet flavors of peach and nectarine finish with a note of apricot.

WINE POACHED PEARS

4 BARTLETT PEARS, PEELED, CORED AND HALVED

1 BOTTLE GEWÜRTZTRAINER

2 CUPS WATER

¾ CUP SUGAR

2 STRIPS LEMON ZEST

2 TBSP FRESH LEMON JUICE

6 BLACK PEPPERCORNS

To make the wine poached pears, place the wine, sugar, lemon zest, lemon juice, peppercorns and water in a pan large enough to hold the pears in one layer.

Bring the pears and liquid to a boil and reduce to a simmer. Simmer gently until a knife pierces the thickest part of the pear, about 15 minutes.

Remove the pears to a platter.

Bring the poaching liquid to a boil and reduce by ⅔, about 20 minutes. Strain the liquid and pour over the pears. Let cool.

Leftover pears can be cooled in their liquid and served with a dollop of crème fraîche.

BLEU CHEESE QUENELLES

⅓ LB HUMBOLDT OR ANY BLEU CHEESE

¼ LB CREAM CHEESE

¼ CUP HEAVY CREAM, WHIPPED

To make the bleu cheese quenelles, purée the cheeses in a food processor until smooth. Season with salt and pepper to taste. Fold the whipped cream into the cheeses until well blended.

Quenelles can be piped onto the soup with a pastry bag or formed with two spoons.

NOTE: To form the quenelles using two spoons, dip a tablespoon into water. Scoop up the mousse and round the tops. Using the other spoon, scoop the mousse from the first spoon, following the curved shape (like a tiny football). Repeat, changing spoons as many times as you need to in order to have a neat, well-shaped quenelle.

ITALIAN STUFFED MEATLOAF

SERVES 6 | PREP TIME: 10 MINUTES | COOK TIME: 1 HOUR 15 MINUTES

- 1 LB LEAN GROUND BEEF
- 1 LB LEAN GROUND PORK
- 2 CUPS + 3 TBSP FRESH BREAD CRUMBS
- 1 CUP GRATED PARMESAN
- 3 LARGE EGGS, BEATEN
- SALT AND PEPPER
- 8 OZ FRESH SPINACH
- 2 CARROTS, CUT LENGTHWISE INTO 6 SLICES EACH (A MANDOLINE WORKS BEST)
- 3 TBSP FLOUR
- 6 SLICES PROSCIUTTO
- 6 OZ PROVOLONE
- 2 SPRIGS FRESH ROSEMARY
- 1 CUP WATER
- ¼ CUP OLIVE OIL

Combine the pork, beef and 2 cups of bread crumbs, Parmesan, eggs, salt and pepper to taste. Mix gently and refrigerate.

Preheat oven to 400°F.

Bring 6 quarts of water to a boil in a large pot and add 1 tbsp salt. Plunge the spinach leaves into the boiling water just until wilted and quickly remove them. Add the carrots to the water and cook for 10 minutes, drain and reserve.

Combine the flour with the remaining 3 tbsp bread crumbs and use this to dust a work surface. Pat the meat mixture into a ½ inch thick rectangle about 16 × 6 inches on the prepared work surface. Lay the spinach leaves over the meat, leaving a 1 inch border on the short sides. Lay the carrot slices over the spinach, lengthwise down the rectangle. Then layer the prosciutto and provolone over the carrots. Starting from a long side, roll into a loaf, making it very compact. Dust the outside with flour.

Place the loaf on a rack in a pan. Put the rosemary under the rack and pour the water into the pan. Pour the olive oil down the length of the loaf. Bake for 1 hour, or until an instant thermometer registers 165°F.

Remove from oven and transfer the loaf to a cutting board. Pour the pan juices into a saucepan and bring to a boil. Season with salt and pepper to taste.

Slice the meat loaf into 1 inch slices and drizzle with the pan juices.

"As you slice this loaf, the brilliant colors of carrot, spinach and prosciutto appear, making it a vibrant dish to whet any appetite."

WINE PAIRING: Danza del Sol Winery | Petite Sirah | Rich Fruit and dark chocolate flavors with a tannic texture finish.

DOFFO WINERY

MARCELO DOFFO PIPES IN ITALIAN CLASSICAL MUSIC TO NUTURE HIS GRAPES.

Marcelo Doffo never intended to own a commercial vineyard and winery. However, his love and dedication to the art of cultivation began as a small child growing up on his grandfather's land in Pampas, Argentina. As a young man, Marcelo emigrated from his grandfather's farmlands in Argentina to the United States where he made a career in car sales and repair.

Marcelo first became interested in winemaking in the mid-1990s, when he visited relatives in Italy and observed them making wine in their basement. Marcelo returned to his home in Orange County eager to see if he too had what it took to make excellent wine. By 1997, Marcelo had created a wine worthy of a silver medal from the Orange County Wine Society.

This honor led Marcelo to purchase an old cattle ranch in Temecula, where he worked tirelessly to prepare the vineyard for planting. His first vines included Cabernet Sauvignon, Syrah, Petite Verdot and Cabernet Franc. Giving a special musical touch to nurture his grapes, Marcelo pipes in Italian classical music to the vines.

Today, Marcelo's son Damian and daughters Brigitte and Samantha continue the Doffo Winery legacy by making small batches of wine that are robust and full of flavor. They produce about 5,000 cases of wine a year.

ARANCINI

MAKES 12 TO 14 ARANCINI | PREP TIME: 70 MINUTES | COOK TIME: 4 MINUTES

6 CUPS PRE-COOKED ARBORIO RICE (THE VERY BEST THING TO USE IS LEFTOVER RISOTTO, SEE WILD MUSHROOM RISOTTO, 81)

6 EGGS (SEPERATE 4 EGGS)

1 CUP PECORINO OR PARMESAN CHEESE, GRATED

1 BUNCH MINT, COARSELY CHOPPED (2 TBSP RESERVED FOR GARNISH)

½ LB PROVOLONE OR MOZZARELLA CHEESE, CUT INTO ½ INCH DICE

1 CUP FLOUR

2 CUPS BREAD CRUMBS

OLIVE OIL, VEGETABLE OIL OR CANOLA OIL (ENOUGH TO POUR 4 INCHES TO THE PAN FOR FRYING)

SALT

1 CUP PARMESAN CHEESE, GRATED FOR GARRNISH

SIMPLE TOMATO SAUCE (RECIPE ON PAGE 120)

Place the cooked rice in a large mixing bowl. Add 2 whole eggs and 4 egg yolks. Mix in Pecorino or Parmesan cheese, salt and mint.

Form the mixture into 2 ½ to 3 inch balls, filling center of the ball with a piece of provolone or mozzarella cheese.

In each of three shallow bowls, place flour, egg whites and bread crumbs. Whisk the egg whites to loosen them. Roll each ball first in flour, then in egg whites, then in bread crumbs. Place balls on a tray and refrigerate uncovered for one hour.

Heat 4 inches of oil in a pot to 375°F.

Carefully place a few balls at a time into the pot and fry until golden brown, about 3 to 4 minutes. Stir to keep them moving. Drain cooked balls on paper towels. Serve hot or at room temperature with Simple Tomato Sauce, recipe on page 120. Garnish with Parmesan cheese and mint.

NOTE: A staple in the Italian kitchen—these are at their best when eaten immediately.

WINE PAIRING: Doffo Winery | Zinfandel | This wine has a brilliant ruby color, with aromas of plum, raspberry, berry jam, violets, and hints of black pepper and vanilla with a soft finish.

SIMPLE TOMATO SAUCE

SERVES 6 | PREP TIME: 10 MINUTES | COOK TIME: 25 MINUTES

- 2 TBSP OLIVE OIL
- 1 LARGE ONION, CHOPPED
- 2 CLOVES GARLIC, MINCED
- 2 (28 OZ) CANS TOMATOES, PUT THROUGH A FOOD MILL OR FINELY CHOPPED
- SALT AND PEPPER
- ½ CUP BASIL LEAVES, CHOPPED
- ¼ CUP SMALL CAPERS (OPTIONAL)

Sauté the onion and garlic in the olive oil.

Add the tomatoes and simmer for 20 minutes.

Stir in the basil and capers just before serving.

"This is a very basic tomato sauce and can be used as a dipping sauce for Arancini (recipe on page 119) but, can also serve as, a basic sauce for pasta."

"I LEARNED THIS FROM AN ITALIAN FRIEND. AFTER TASTING THE SAUCE, IF IT SEEMS TOO ACIDIC, SPRINKLE IN A LITTLE SUGAR TO ROUND IT OUT."

ROAST LEG OF LAMB WITH ARTICHOKES

SERVES 8 | PREP TIME: 20 MINUTES | COOK TIME: 1 HOUR 30 MINUTES

1 (4 TO 5 LB) LEG OF LAMB, BUTTERFLIED

1 SMALL LEMON

2 CLOVES GARLIC, PEELED AND SLIVERED

4 SPRIGS FRESH DILL

½ TSP DRIED OREGANO

4 FRESH ARTICHOKES

2 LB SMALL NEW POTATOES

Preheat oven to 425°F.

Place lamb, fat side up in large shallow roasting pan. Remove the zest from the lemon and cut into thin strips. Make small slits all over the leg of lamb and insert a sliver of lemon, garlic and dill in each slit. Sprinkle the lamb with salt and oregano.

Roast in oven for 15 minutes, then lower heat to 350°F and continue cooking for 30 minutes.

Meanwhile, trim stalk from base of the artichokes, cut a slice from the top leaves and snip off ends of spiky leaves. Halve the artichokes and scrape out the choke. Rub all surfaces with lemon juice. Parboil 5 minutes in boiling salted water, then drain.

Pare a ring of skin from the middle of each potato. They will soak up the flavors of the pan juices if not completely covered in skin.

After cooking the lamb for the first 45 minutes, add the artichokes and potatoes to the roasting pan with the lamb. Roast about 55 minutes longer or until an instant thermometer registers 140°F for medium.

Let the lamb rest for 10 minutes, then slice and serve with the potatoes and artichokes.

"Lamb is one of my favorite meats and if you're undecided about it, try it with these artichokes, which are cooked in the juices of the roasting meat."

WINE PAIRING: Doffo Winery | Malbec | The ruby red color has aromas of strawberry with hints of vanilla, coffee, and tobacco. It has bright acidity and fine oak tannins.

EUROPA VILLAGE

"WE EXTEND A NEW INVITATION TO EXPERIENCE OLD WORLD CHARM."
— Europa Village Winery

In 2006, owner Dan Stephenson purchased over 300 acres of land at the entrance of Temecula Wine Country and his plan to build a multi-winery resort representing France, Italy and Spain, his favorite wine producing countries, was set in motion.

Europa Village combines Old World hospitality and charm with vibrant colors, bold flavors and exquisite shopping, staying, and dining experiences. They are committed to producing wines that are truly works of art and approach winemaking with all the "talent, expertise and meticulous attention to detail that fine artists apply to the creation of their masterpieces." Their acclaimed Bolero restaurant presents a world-class culinary experience.

Europa Village winemakers handcraft premium estate wines inspired by the Old World traditions of France, Spain, and Italy. The resulting wines have enticing aromas, rich colors and smooth finishes. Europa Village strives to make classic wines with elegance, balance and distinctive bouquets and flavors. It is these qualities that make Europa Village wines memorable and entice guests to return time and time again.

Europa Village produces 12,000 cases of reds, whites, rosés and sparkling wines a year.

EUROPA VILLAGE
LA SCAPPATELLA
"THE ESCAPE"
PREMIUM CALIFORNIA
SPARKLING WINE
Bolero
CELLARS
2016
MUSCAT CANELLI
Vienza
SANGIOVESE
EUROPA VILLAGE
C'est La Vie
2014
SYRAH
PRIVATE RESERVE
Estate Wine • Temecula Valley

WINTER BEEF AND VEGETABLE SOUP

SERVES 6 TO 8 | PREP TIME: 15 MINUTES | COOK TIME: 1 HOUR 30 MINUTES

- 2 TBSP OLIVE OIL
- 1 LB BEEF CHUCK, CUT INTO 1 INCH PIECES
- 6 CUPS BEEF STOCK
- 1 LARGE ONION, CHOPPED
- 2 CELERY STALKS, CHOPPED
- 2 RED-SKINNED POTATOES, SKIN ON, CUT INTO 1 INCH PIECES
- 1 (28 OZ) CAN CRUSHED PLUM TOMATOES WITH JUICES
- ½ LB GREEN BEANS, TRIMMED
- 2 TBSP ITALIAN PARSLEY, CHOPPED
- SALT AND PEPPER

Season beef with salt and pepper.

Add 1 tbsp oil to a large saucepan and brown the beef. Remove and reserve.

Add the remaining 1 tbsp oil to the saucepan and reduce the heat to medium. Add the onion, carrots and celery. Cover the pan and cook, stirring occasionally, until the onion is translucent. Return the beef and juices to the pan.

Add the beef stock to the pan. Bring to a boil. Reduce the heat and simmer partially covered, for 1 hour. Add the potatoes and tomatoes. Simmer until the beef and potatoes are tender, about 10 minutes. Add the green beans and cook 5 more minutes. Season with salt and pepper

Serve in a bowl and sprinkle with fresh parsley.

"Winter and fall, a hearty soup accompanied by bread, wine and a place by the fireside is a great answer to 'What's for Dinner.'"

WINE PAIRING: Europa Village | Tempranillo | This wine mixes fruit, spice and barrel flavors with aromas of spices and black cherry.

CHEESE SOUFFLÉ

SERVES 4 TO 6 | PREP TIME: 10 MINUTES | COOK TIME: 30 MINUTES

- 3 TBSP UNSALTED BUTTER + ADDITIONAL TO COAT SOUFFLÉ MOLD
- 3 TBSP FLOUR + ADDITIONAL TO COAT SOUFFLÉ MOLD
- 1 CUP WHOLE MILK
- ½ TSP SALT
- DASH PEPPER
- DASH NUTMEG
- 4 LARGE EGGS, SEPARATED + 3 ADDITIONAL EGG WHITES
- ¾ CUP GRUYERE OR EMMENTHAL (SWISS) CHEESE, GRATED

Butter a 1 ½ quart soufflé mold. Sprinkle flour, rolling it around so that it coats the soufflé dish. Refrigerate the mold.

Preheat the oven to 400°F.

Melt the butter in a saucepan over low heat. Stir in the flour and cook slowly, stirring constantly, until the butter and flour froth (about 3 minutes). Don't let it brown. Take off the heat and add the milk, salt, pepper and nutmeg, whipping constantly with a wire whisk. Return to heat and bring to a boil, still whipping. Take off the heat and cool for 5 minutes. Add the egg yolks, one at a time, whisking after each addition.

With an electric mixer or whisk, whip the 7 egg whites until they hold firm peaks. Beat in ⅓ of the egg whites into the yolk mixture. Add the grated cheese and mix in. Fold in the remaining egg whites.

Pour the batter into the prepared mold, smooth the top with a spatula. Put into the oven and bake for 20 to 25 minutes.

"Soufflés are great because I usually have the ingredients on hand. It's a good place to use up bits of leftover cheese. Preparing soufflés couldn't be easier and that is a well kept secret!"

WINE PAIRING: Europa Village | Sangiovese | Strawberry, cedarwood and black tea on the nose. Elegant on the palate, with vibrant tannins on the finish.

SEAFOOD TACOS

SERVES 6 | PREP TIME: 30 MINUTES | COOK TIME: 15 MINUTES

MARINADE

1 ANCHO CHILE, SEEDED

¼ TSP CUMIN

1 TSP SALT

1 TBSP HONEY

1 TBSP SOY SAUCE

¾ CUP ORANGE JUICE

¼ TSP BLACK PEPPER

¼ TSP GARLIC POWDER

¼ TSP ALLSPICE

TACOS

1 LB COD OR OTHER WHITE FISH

½ LB SHRIMP, PEELED AND DEVEINED

3 TBSP OLIVE OIL

12 CORN TORTILLAS

SPICY CABBAGE

LIME AIOLI

AVOCADO, DICED

To make the marinade, place all ingredients in a saucepan and bring to a simmer. When the chile is softened, take the pan off the heat and cool. Pour into a blender and purée.

Chop the seafood into 1 inch cubes and put it into the marinade. Refrigerate until ready to cook.

To make the tacos, drain the marinated seafood. Heat the olive oil in a sauté pan, add the seafood and sauté until the seafood is opaque and cooked through.

Just before the seafood is done cooking, coat a skillet with oil and lightly fry the corn tortillas.

To serve, spoon the seafood onto the hot tortillas.

Serve with lime aioli and spicy cabbage, recipe on page 132.

WINE PAIRING: Europa Village | Albariño | Aromas of white peach, lime, lemon and nectarine reveal the promise of a Spanish summer breeze.

LIME AIOLI AND SPICY CABBAGE

MAKES 1 ½ CUPS | PREP TIME: 10 MINUTES

LIME AIOLI

1 TSP SALT

1 TSP SUGAR

¼ TSP BLACK PEPPER

2 CLOVES GARLIC, PEELED

2 EGG YOLKS

¼ CUP LIME JUICE

1 ⅓ CUP OLIVE OIL

2 TSP WATER

SPICY CABBAGE

3 CUPS CABBAGE, SHREDDED

1 TBSP CHOLULA BRAND HOT SAUCE

1 TSP BLACK PEPPER

1 TSP SALT

3 TBSP APPLE CIDER VINEGAR

1 TBSP OLIVE OIL

½ TSP SUGAR

To make the lime aioli, place salt, sugar, pepper, garlic, egg yolks and lime juice in a blender and purée. With the blender at medium speed add the oil very slowly. Add 1 to 2 tsp water and mix. You can add more water if it is too thick for drizzling.

To make the spicy cabbage, mix all ingredients together.

Serve with the seafood tacos, recipe on page 130.

"THE SPICY MARINADE LENDS GREAT FLAVOR TO THE WHITE FISH AND THE SPICY CABBAGE WITH AIOLI GARNISH IS A SURPRISING VARIATION ON A MEXICAN DISH. SPARKLING WINE IS MY CHOICE TO ACCOMPANY THIS."

TARTE GRAND-MÈRE

SERVES 6 TO 8 | PREP TIME: 20 MINUTES | COOK TIME: 30 MINUTES

DOUGH

1 ¼ CUPS ALL PURPOSE FLOUR

8 TBSP SWEET BUTTER, CHILLED AND CUT INTO ¼ INCH BITS

⅛ TSP SALT

¼ TSP SUGAR

3 TBSP ICE WATER

FILLING

2 TO 3 APPLES

3 TBSP SUGAR

2 TBSP SWEET BUTTER

GLAZE

3 TBSP APRICOT JAM

1 TBSP BRANDY OR ORANGE LIQUEUR

To make the dough, place flour, salt and butter into the bowl of a food processor. Pulse until the flour mixture is incorporated and resembles corn meal. While motor is running, add ice water. Pulse until the dough collects into a ball in the machine. Pour out onto a floured surface and shape into a disk, about 4 inches in diameter. Wrap in plastic and refrigerate for 30 minutes.

Preheat oven to 400°F.

To make the filling, peel, core and thinly slice the apples.

Line a baking sheet with parchment. Roll out prepared dough into a circle, about 12 inches in diameter. Transfer dough to the baking sheet. Arrange apple slices on the dough, overlapping the slices leaving 1 inch uncovered all around the edge. Fold the 1 inch of dough over the apples. Sprinkle sugar over apples and dot with the butter.

Bake in oven for 25 to 30 minutes.

To make the glaze, heat jam and liqueur until the jam melts. Strain mixture through a sieve and brush over apple tart.

To serve, cut tarte into wedges and top with a dollop of whipped cream.

"I've been making this simple country tart for decades. A variation on the usual apple pie done in a pie tin, this tart is pretty and stars the flaky crust and delicious fresh apples."

WINE PAIRING: Europa Village | Muscat Canelli | Aromas and flavors of peach, apricot and orange blossom with a nicely balanced residual sugar.

FALKNER WINERY

"I AM DRAWN TO THE ATTENTION TO DETAIL AND QUALITY AT FALKNER. I LIKE TO BE INVOLVED IN THE VINEYARD TO KNOW WHAT I'M GETTING BECAUSE THE POTENTIAL IS ESTABLISHED IN THE VINEYARD, AND THEN IT'S MY JOB TO CREATE A SUPERIOR PRODUCT."

— Duncan Williams, winemaker, Falkner Winery

Owners Ray and Loretta Falkner purchased the winery in 2000, with the vineyards originally planted in 1975 and used by Britton Cellars, Clos du Muriel, and Temecula Crest Wineries. Together with winemakers Steve Hagata, now retired, and Duncan Williams, the Falkners have taken the wine business to a new level with their production of high-quality Mediterranean style wines including Chardonnay, Cabernet Sauvignon, Riesling, Sauvignon Blanc, Syrah, Merlot, Meritage, Viognier, and their own proprietary blended wines like Amante, a robust, Super Tuscan style red wine.

Falkner Winery produces premium wines with outstanding varietal character from grapes that are grown on the estate. Eighty percent of the wines on their menu have received gold or silver medals and 12 have received 90+ ratings from Wine Enthusiast magazine. They produce 7,000 cases of wine a year.

FALKNER
FALKNER
WINERY
Viognier
TEMECULA VALLEY

SPAGHETTI WITH WHITE CLAM SAUCE

SERVES 4 TO 6 | PREP TIME: 10 MINUTES | COOK TIME: 20 MINUTES

1 LB SPAGHETTI

2 TBSP OLIVE OIL

3 OZ PANCETTA, CHOPPED

½ CUP ONIONS, FINELY CHOPPED

3 TBSP GARLIC, THINLY SLICED

2 TSP FRESH OREGANO, CHOPPED

½ TSP SALT

¼ TSP CRUSHED RED PEPPER FLAKES (OPTIONAL)

2 LB LITTLE NECK CLAMS, COCKLES OR VENUS CLAMS, PURGED AND SCRUBBED

¾ CUP DRY WHITE WINE

½ CUP CLAM JUICE

½ CUP HEAVY CREAM

2 TSP FRESH LEMON JUICE

BEURRE MANIÉ (1 TBSP FLOUR AND 1 TBSP ROOM TEMP BUTTER WORKED WITH YOUR HANDS INTO A PASTE)

¼ CUP PARSLEY, CHOPPED (FOR GARNISH)

½ CUP PARMESAN, FINELY GRATED (FOR GARNISH)

Fill a large pot with salted water and bring to a boil. Add spaghetti and cook al dente. Strain, run under cold water and set aside

In a heavy sauté pan heat the oil. Add the pancetta and cook, stirring for 2 minutes. Add the onions and garlic and cook for 2 minutes. Add the oregano, salt and red pepper flakes and cook for 1 minute. Add the wine and clam juice and cook for 1 minute. Add the clams, cover and shake occasionally. Cook until all the clams are open, about 5 minutes. Remove the clams and put on a platter while you finish the sauce. Discard any unopened ones.

Add the cream and lemon juice and simmer for 1 minute. Whisk in the beurre manié and cook for a minute or two or until the sauce is slightly thickened. Put the clams back into the pan to warm.

Toss with spaghetti and garnish with parsley and olive oil. Serve with Parmesan cheese.

"Only fresh clams will do for this pasta dish. Serve the pasta in a flat rimmed soup dish. If you wish, some of the meat can be taken out of the shells and added to the pasta leaving several clams in the shells for serving."

WINE PAIRING: Falkner Winery | Viognier | This wine is pale colored with slightly tropical flavors. It is a dry, easy drinking wine and has great white peach, honeysuckle, citrus, and white flower flavors.

SUMMER STRAWBERRY TART

SERVES 8 TO 10 | PREP TIME: 25 MINUTES | COOK TIME: 45 MINUTES

PÂTE BRISÉE

1 ¼ CUPS ALL PURPOSE FLOUR

8 TBSP UNSALTED BUTTER

⅛ TSP SALT

¼ TSP SUGAR

3 TBSP COLD WATER

CRÈME PÂTISSIÈRE

4 EGG YOLKS

⅓ CUP SUGAR

1 TSP VANILLA

2 TBSP CORNSTARCH

1 ¼ CUPS MILK

FINISH

2 CUPS FRESH STRAWBERRIES, THINLY SLICED ON THE VERTICAL

¼ CUP CURRANT JELLY MIXED WITH A LITTLE FRUIT LIQUOR

To make the pâte brisée, cut butter into flour, salt and sugar using a pastry cutter, your fingers or a food processor. Add the water and mix rapidly. Empty bowl onto floured surface and form into a disk the size of a Brie cheese, approximately 6 inches. Refrigerate for 30 minutes.

Preheat oven to 400°F.

Roll out the dough into the shape of your pan with a 1 inch overlap. Place it in the tart pan, roll over the edges and crimp. Line the bottom of the pastry with aluminum foil and weight the shell with beans, rice or pie weights. Bake for 20 minutes, remove the pie weights and bake for another 10 minutes. Cool before filling.

To make the créme pâtissière, whisk yolks, sugar and vanilla until it forms a ribbon. Add the cornstarch and mix until blended. Bring the milk to a boil. Pour half the boiling milk into the yolk mixture and whisk until smooth. Pour back into the saucepan and bring to a boil. Pour into a bowl, cover and cool.

When all ingredients are cool spread the pastry cream in the shell. Arrange the sliced berries over the pastry cream starting at the outer edge of the tart and working in to form a wheel pattern.

NOTE: It's prettier to have the points of the berries pointing out.

To make the finish, heat the jelly and the liquor in a small saucepan. Cool a little to avoid cooking the strawberry slices and brush over the top of the tart. Refrigerate tart.

Serve as soon as possible, this tart does not keep well.

WINE PAIRING: Falkner Winery | Risqué Riesling | This semi-dry white wine has a wonderful ripe pear flavor followed by spices such as nutmeg and cinnamon.

FAZELI CELLARS

"OUR ROOTS RUN DEEP" — Fazeli Cellars

In 2001, when the Fazeli family decided to visit the Temecula Valley, they fell in love with the area and purchased land to "grow some grapes and maybe make a little wine."

That same year, they founded Fazeli Cellars. Bizhan "BJ" Fazelli chose the Shiraz grape as the benchmark varietal for his winery, producing its first vintage in 2006. From the start, Fazeli Cellars has paid homage to the rich cultural heritage of Ancient Persia and has made a commitment to excellence and the production of quality wines that often tell a story. Each wine's name is unique, carefully considered and "bears a meaningful connection to Fazeli's Persian heritage."

Today, Fazeli Cellars is a state-of-the-art winery with a fine selection of boutique wines "honoring ancient traditions of Persia rooted in a modern expression of California." The cellar's collection has grown to twenty varietals which include, Cabernet Sauvignon, Sauvignon Blanc, Petite Sirah, Mourvedre, Viognier, Chardonnay, and Shiraz. Their red wines are aged in French, Hungarian and American oak barrels. Fazeli Cellars produces 10-12,000 cases of wine a year.

Inspired by the ancient traditions of Persia.
Rooted in the modern expressions of California.
Fazeli
CELLARS
Ruby Rose
DRY ROSÉ WINE
TEMECULA VALLEY, CA

SEAFOOD SALAD PARFAIT WITH AVOCADO

SERVES 6 | PREP TIME: 10 MINUTES | COOK TIME: 0 MINUTES

½ LB SMALL SHRIMP, COOKED, PEELED AND DEVEINED

2 TBSP MAYONNAISE

1 LEMON, JUICED AND RIND GRATED

3 TBSP RED BELL PEPPER, DICED

2 TBSP FRESH CHIVES, CHOPPED

3 TBSP ENGLISH CUCUMBER, DICED

1 DASH HOT SAUCE

8 OZ LUMP CRAB MEAT

1 LARGE RIPE AVOCADO, DICED

MICROGREENS, CHOPPED PARSLEY OR WATERCRESS

Combine the shrimp, mayonnaise, juice of one lemon, bell pepper, chives, cucumber and hot sauce. Mix in the crabmeat just before serving.

In a parfait glass, put a few microgreens and add a layer of the seafood mixture.

Put a layer of avocado, then another layer of the seafood.

Top the dish with a few microgreens and a smidgeon of lemon rind.

This is very pretty served as an appetizer or first course in tall slender glasses as pictured.

WINE PAIRING: Fazeli Cellars | Sauvignon Blanc | Bracingly fresh, with a nose that is sweetly grassy and a hint of citrus, followed by a touch of sour apple and lengthy finish. Crisp and clean palate.

SMOKED SALMON PIZZA

MAKES 2 (10 INCH) PIZZAS | PREP TIME: 60 MINUTES | COOK TIME: 10 MINUTES

PIZZA DOUGH

1 TBSP GRANULATED SUGAR

1 CUP WARM (110 TO 115°F) WATER

1 ENVELOPE ACTIVE DRY YEAST

3 ½ CUPS BREAD FLOUR OR UNBLEACHED FLOUR

1 TSP SALT

¼ CUP OLIVE OIL

1 BAKED PIZZA CRUST

4 OZ SMOKED SALMON

6 TO 8 OZ CRÈME FRAÎCHE

2 TSP CAPERS

1 TO 2 TBSP FRESH DILL, CHOPPED

To make the pizza dough, in a small bowl dissolve sugar in water and sprinkle yeast over the top. Stir gently until it dissolves.

Add 3 cups of flour and the salt to the bowl of a food processor. Using the steel blade, combine ingredients. Add yeast mixture and oil and process continuously until the dough forms a single ball on top of the blade, about 30 seconds.

Turn out onto a lightly floured surface and knead by hand for about 2 minutes.

Place in a well oiled bowl, cover and let rise until doubled, about 1 to 1 ½ hours.

Preheat oven to 450°F.

Punch dough down and pour out onto a lightly floured surface. Divide into two balls and proceed to roll out dough with a rolling pin or stretch with your hands.

Place pizza dough on a pizza peel and bake in oven on a pizza stone for about 10 minutes. Check often and move pizza around with the pizza peel until crispy and brown on the edges. Let cool for 5 minutes before adding toppings. Repeat with the second ball of dough.

To prepare the pizza, spread crème fraîche on a cooled crust. Layer thin slices of salmon over the crème fraîche.

Distribute the capers over the top and sprinkle the dill over everything.

WINE PAIRING: Fazeli Cellars | Ruby Rosé | Bright strawberry and cherry flavors with crisp acid and rounding sweetness.

STUFFED CABBAGE

SERVES 6 | PREP TIME: 25 MINUTES | COOK TIME: 35 MINUTES

- 1 HEAD CABBAGE
- 8 OZ GROUND BEEF
- 3 OZ BACON, BLANCHED AND CHOPPED
- 3 OZ MUSHROOMS, CHOPPED
- 1 CLOVE GARLIC, FINELY MINCED
- 2 TSP EACH FRESH PARSLEY, SAGE, ROSEMARY, THYME AND CHIVES
- 2 CUPS BREAD CRUMBS
- 2 WHOLE EGGS, WHISKED
- ¼ TSP NUTMEG
- SALT AND PEPPER

Bring a large pot of water to a boil.

Insert a large fork all the way into the core end of the cabbage.

Submerge the cabbage in the boiling water for 2 to 3 minutes, rotating it from side to side, until the outer leaves are softened. Remove cabbage from boiling water and peel away several layers of the outer leaves, being careful to leave them attached.

Let the cabbage cool and drain. Remove the core of the cabbage creating a pocket for the stuffing.

For the stuffing, combine the remaing ingredients. The consistency should be like an uncooked meatloaf.

Fill the cabbage with the stuffing and push the outer leaves back into shape to encase the filling.

Wrap the cabbage securely in cheese cloth and set aside.

To make the broth, add butter to a large pot and sauté the onions. Stir in the flour. Add the stock and herb bundle. When the broth is at boiling, turn down the heat and add the stuffed cabbage. Cook for about 35 to 40 minutes or until tender.

Remove cabbage from broth and allow excess broth to drain. To serve, place the stuffed cabbage on a platter and slice into wedges. This can also be served in a rimmed soup bowl with some of the broth spooned over the cabbage wedge.

WINE PAIRING: Fazeli Cellars | Shiraz | Flavors of black currant and blackberry with hints of vanilla and black pepper.

BROTH

1 MEDIUM ONION, SLICED

2 TBSP BUTTER

2 QUARTS CHICKEN OR BEEF BROTH TO COVER THE CABBAGE WHILE COOKING

1 BUNDLE FRESH HERBS TIED TOGETHER (THYME, SAGE, ROSEMARY, TARRAGON OR ANY COMBINATION)

3 TBSP FLOUR

"A delicious old-fashioned dish that says comfort food and warms up a winter day."

FOOT PATH WINERY

"WE CRAFT OUR WINES NATURALLY, BECAUSE NATURE KNOWS BEST."
— Deane Foote, owner and winemaker, Foot Path Winery

Winemaker Deane Foote and his wife Christine, the "estate monarch," own and operate the family farm and vineyard founded in 2005. Their vineyard is the only one in the Temecula Valley with 100% certified organic and non-GMO grapes. They also grow organic citrus, pomegranates and figs, which are sold in their tasting room alongside their handcrafted red wines and organic honey. Their wines are low sulfite, low in tannins, "unfiltered, unadulterated, and unmatched."

Their winery is informal. Their goal is to keep it simple, have fun, and enjoy limited quantities of handcrafted red wines made by the Foote family. In this spirit, when you join their wine club, you are not just becoming another wine member, but a member of their family.

The Foote Family says, "When you visit us, you are visiting our family farm." They invite folks to "take the road less traveled" and say, "You're always on the right path when you're drinking Foot Path wines".

Foot Path Winery produces about 500 cases of wine a year. Deane and Christine say their wines "are for seekers of quality wine without pretense."

Foot Path
Winery
FP
2016
Cabernet Sauvignon
Temecula Valley
Produced and Bottled By
Foot Path Winery Temecula, CA

FRENCH ONION SOUP

SERVES 8 | PREP TIME: 10 MINUTES | COOK TIME: 1 HOUR 20 MINUTES COOK TIME FOR BEEF STOCK: 6 HOURS)

BEEF STOCK

4 LB BEEF BONES

1 ONION, ROUGHLY CHOPPED

2 CARROTS, ROUGHLY CHOPPED

1 BAY LEAF

1 TSP BLACK PEPPERCORNS

2 TSP SALT

2 LB ONIONS, THINLY SLICED

6 TBSP BUTTER

2 QUARTS BEEF STOCK (SEE ABOVE, CAN USE PREPARED BUT FLAVORS ARE NOT AS GOOD)

8 SLICES FRENCH BREAD, CUT INTO ½ INCH SLICES

2 CUPS GRUYERE CHEESE, GRATED

SALT AND PEPPER

To make the beef stock, preheat oven to 450°F.

Place the bones, onion and carrots in a roasting pan and roast until dark brown, not burned.

Place the bone mixture into a stock kettle and cover with cold water. Bring to a boil, skimming any scum that forms at the surface. When the mixture comes to a boil, lower the heat and simmer slowly for 6 hours. Strain. Let cool and remove the fat that has accumulated from the top. The beef stock can be frozen for latter use.

To make the soup, melt the butter in a large saucepan and add the sliced onions. Cook on low heat until the onions are caramelized, stirring frequently. This can take up to 45 minutes and should not be rushed. The caramelization is what gives the soup its rich flavor.

Add the beef stock and simmer for 30 to 40 minutes.

Preheat oven to 350°F.

Put the slices of bread on a baking sheet and spray with olive oil.

Bake for 10 minutes, turn and bake for another 10 minutes.

Set the oven to broil.

Season soup with salt and pepper to taste. Ladle the soup into individual oven proof bowls and float a crouton on top. Sprinkle with the Gruyere cheese and place the bowls under the broiler, checking constantly. The cheese should be melted onto the crouton. Serve piping hot.

WINE PAIRING: Foot Path Winery | Cabernet Sauvignon | A well made wine with 14% alcohol with a finish of oak and black cherry.

CHOCOLATE PEAR TART

MAKES 1 (10 INCH) TART | PREP TIME: 20 MINUTES | COOK TIME: 40 MINUTES

TART SHELL

8 TBSP BUTTER

1 ½ CUPS FLOUR

1 EGG

½ CUP SUGAR

½ CUP COCOA POWDER

CHOCOLATE FILLING

½ CUP SEMI-SWEET CHOCOLATE, CHOPPED INTO SMALL BITS

4 TBSP BUTTER

2 EGGS

⅓ CUP SUGAR

FILLING

2 MEDIUM FRESH PEARS, PEELED, CORED AND SLICED LENGTHWISE

2 TBSP ORANGE MARMALADE

To make the tart shell, preheat oven to 350°F.

Put the flour, sugar and cocoa into a food processor. Pulse until mixed, then add the butter and pulse until the mixture looks like corn meal. Add the egg and process until the mixture comes away from the blades and gathers into a ball on the side of the bowl. Line a tart pan with a removable bottom with the dough.

To make the chocolate filling, put the chocolate and butter in a heat proof bowl and place in bain-marie (double boiler). When the chocolate mixture is melted, take the bowl out of the bain-marie and allow to cool.

Separate the eggs. Beat the whites until they hold stiff peaks and reserve.

In a seperate bowl, mix the egg yolks and sugar and beat thoroughly. Stir in the chocolate and fold in the egg whites.

To assemble, spread the marmalade on the bottom of the dough. Arrange the sliced pears on the dough. Pour the chocolate filling over the pears and bake for about 40 minutes.

"This is an unusual pairing of chocolate and fresh pears and something I enjoyed in Tuscany."

WINE PAIRING: Foot Path Winery | Late Harvest Zinfandel | A bold wine with a smooth and silky texture produced by fine craftsmanship and a lengthy aging process.

FRANGIPANI ESTATE WINERY

"WE REALLY TRY TO JUST GET PEOPLE TO SLOW DOWN MORE THAN ANYTHING." — Don Frangipani, owner and winemaker, Frangipani Estate Winery

The Frangipani Estate Winery label was established in 2003, the Temecula Valley property was purchased in 2005, and its tasting room opened in 2006. Frangipani Estate Winery sits atop a plateau overlooking a breathtaking view of the Temecula Valley. Adding a dynamic selection of wines gives guests an unparalleled euphoric experience. Don invites his guests to "slow down" and enjoy the wines and the view.

Don Frangipani's love for fine wines and the Temecula Valley developed while working at the Cilurzo Winery in 1995. There, he perfected his art and built on his own unique style to create bold red wines and crisp, clean white wines. Don and JoAnn Frangipani have been in farming for over three decades and are no strangers to hard work and perseverance. They produce wines from the French varietals of Cabernet Franc, Malbec, Cabernet Sauvignon, and Petite Verdot and combine them with Old World Italian styles to create a distinctive collection of wines. Other estate grown varietals are Sangiovese, Grenache, and Petite Syrah.

Frangipani Estate Winery currently produces 5,000 cases of wine a year.

FRANGIPANI
ESTATE
WINERY
2013
Claret
TEMECULA VALLEY
alcohol 13.9% by vol.

CORNED BEEF WITH CLARET GLAZE

SERVES 8 | PREP TIME: 15 MINUTES | COOK TIME: 4 TO 5 HOURS

CORNED BEEF

3 LB CORNED BEEF BRISKET, BRINED, UNCOOKED

2 BAY LEAVES

2 TSP WHOLE BLACK PEPPERCORNS

4 ALLSPICE BERRIES

2 WHOLE CLOVES

16 CUPS COLD WATER

12 CARROTS, PEELED AND HALVED LENGTHWISE

GLAZE

1 CUP ORANGE MARMALADE

½ CUP CLARET

⅛ TSP NUTMEG

1 TBSP DIJON MUSTARD

Rinse the corned beef in cold water.

Put the corned beef in a large Dutch oven with a lid and add the water, bay leaves, peppercorns, allspice and cloves. Bring to a boil and skim off any scum that rises to the surface. Cover the pan, reduce heat and cook until tender, about 3 to 4 hours.The brisket can also be cooked in a 350°F oven for 3 to 4 hours.

Preheat oven to 425 degrees.

Remove the corned beef from the cooking water and place in a roasting pan. Generously brush the beef with the glaze.

Toss carrots with ¼ cup glaze in a large bowl to coat and place them around the beef.

Roast until the carrots are tender and beef is glazed about 35 minutes, brushing now and then with more glaze.

Serve with additional mustard.

To make the glaze, place the marmalade, claret, nutmeg and mustard in a pan and cook until reduced to ¾ cup of liquid. Stir often. This takes about 5 to 7 minutes.

Corned Beef with Claret Glaze pairs nicely with Roasted New Potatoes and Onions, recipe on page 163. The addition of roasted carrots makes this dish especially colorful and delicious.

WINE PAIRING: Frangipani Estate Winery | Claret | Bordeaux style blend of Cabernet Sauvignon, Malbec, Merlot and Petite Verdot. Flavors of spiced plum, ripe fig, and espresso.

ROASTED NEW POTATOES AND ONIONS

SERVES 6 | PREP TIME: 20 MINUTES | COOK TIME: 25 MINUTES

3 DOZEN BABY POTATOES (ABOUT 1 INCH IN DIAMETER)

1 ½ DOZEN BABY ONIONS, BLANCHED AND PEELED (ABOUT 1 INCH IN DIAMETER)

¼ CUP OLIVE OIL

KOSHER SALT

Preheat oven to 350°F.

Put onions and potatoes into a large bowl and toss with the olive oil and place in a roasting pan.

Roast until a knife point can pierce to the center of the potato and the onions are browned, about 20 to 25 minutes.

Sprinkle with Kosher salt and serve.

Roasted New Potatoes and Onions makes a delicious side dish when paired with Corned Beef with Claret Glaze, recipe on page 160.

ROASTED TOMATO SOUP WITH PUFF PASTRY CAPS

SERVES 6 | PREP TIME: 1 HOUR | COOK TIME: 35 MINUTES

ROASTED TOMATOES

3 LB TOMATOES, CUT IN HALF

1 TBSP OLIVE OIL

2 TBSP BALSAMIC VINEGAR

1 GARLIC CLOVE, MINCED

¼ TSP SALT

¼ TSP PEPPER

½ TSP DRIED THYME

Continued on page 166

To Roast the tomatoes, preheat oven to 350°F.

Place the tomatoes, cut side up on a baking sheet.

Whisk together the olive oil, balsamic vinegar, garlic clove, salt, pepper and thyme. Spoon the mixture evenly over the tomatoes and bake until the tomatoes are soft and the skins are wrinkled, about 1 hour. Remove the skins, reserving any juice.

Continued on page 166.

WINE PAIRING: Frangipani Estate Winery | Malbec | Full bodied with aromas of smoke, plum and blackberry.

SOUP

ROASTED TOMATOES

1 TBSP OLIVE OIL

1 ONION, CHOPPED

½ CUP WHITE WINE

3 CUPS CHICKEN BROTH

1 ½ TSP SUGAR

SALT AND PEPPER

1 CUP CREAM

To make the soup, add the olive oil and the onion to a saucepan and cook until the onion is soft, about 10 minutes. Add the wine, and cook until the wine is evaporated. Add the broth, roasted tomatoes and the juices from the pan that the tomatoes were roasted in. Simmer for 10 minutes.

In a food processor, purée the soup until smooth. Add the sugar, cream and salt and pepper to taste.

Put the hot soup into individual oven proof bowls while you prepare the puff pastry topping..

PUFF PASTRY TOPPING

1 LB PUFF PASTRY

1 EGG

1 TBSP WATER

Preheat oven to 450°F.

To make the puff pastry topping, whisk the egg and the water together.

Cut the puff pastry into rounds about 1 inch wider than the rim of your soup bowls (it also works really well to use pastry cut into squares.).

Gently brush the rounds with the egg wash. Turn the rounds, egg side down, over the tops of the soup bowls. Drape the rounds tightly over the bowls and press along the sides to seal. Brush tops with the egg wash.

Bake in oven for 12 to 15 minutes, or until golden brown.

GERSHON BACHUS VINTNERS

"LIFE'S TOO SHORT TO DRINK BAD WINE."
— Ken and Christina Falik, owners and winemakers, Gershon Bachus Vintners

Gershon Bachus Vintners is a Tuscan-style winery on the DePortola Trail in the Temecula Wine Country. Following in the footsteps of his grandfather Gershon Bachus, who brought his winemaking heritage to America in 1922, Ken Falik and his wife Christina delight in making great wines and sharing it with friends. Together with current lead winemaker Dakota Denton, a lifelong Temecula resident, they encourage wine drinkers to sit down, relax, and allow their senses to be heightened by the great taste of their wines.

Ken and Christina began planting their twenty acres in 2006. They believe in making their wines with love in small batches and produce 3,200 cases of wine a year. Their estate varietals include: Cabernet Franc, Zinfandel, Grenache, Roussanne, Petite Verdot and Cabernet Sauvignon. Their wines are aged in toasted Hungarian or French oak barrels which help to create that long, smooth finish present in many of their award-winning, bold and balanced red wines.

Gershon Bachus Vintners (GBV) is the only winery in the Temecula Valley to produce Kosher-style wines. Their "Hanukkah 8" beautifully handcrafted wine varietals are available, offering a different wine each night during Hanukkah. Of course, these wines and others are perfect every day of the year. Rabbi Marc Rubenstein who is on staff at B'nai Chaim in Murrieta begins the required rituals before bud break, at harvest and through the end of bottling.

The Faliks say, "When you pay close attention to the grapes, giving them every nutrient they need, then the wine takes care of itself".

GERSHON
BACHUS
VINTNERS
MIND SERIES
AEOLUS
2013

SHRIMP SCAMPI IN PUFF PASTRY SHELL

SERVES 8 TO 10 AS AN APPETIZER | PREP TIME: 15 MINUTES | COOK TIME: 25 MINUTES

2 LBS.SHRIMP (31 TO 35S OR 36 TO 40S WOULD BE A GOOD SIZE FOR THIS RECIPE), PEELED AND DEVEINED

3 TBSP OLIVE OIL

1 SMALL ONION, THINLY SLICED

2 TBSP GARLIC, CHOPPED

1 LEMON, JUICED

½ CUP WHITE WINE

2 TBSP BUTTER, COLD

2 TBSP PARSLEY, CHOPPED

SALT AND PEPPER

1 RECIPE LEMON BUTTER SAUCE

8 OZ FROZEN PUFF PASTRY

Continued on page 174

Season the shrimp with salt and pepper.

Add the 3 tbsp of olive oil to a sauté pan. When the pan is hot, add the shrimp.

Quickly sauté until the shrimp just turns pink. Remove from the pan and set aside.

Add the onions and sauté until translucent and add the garlic. Cook for another minute and add the lemon juice and white wine. Reduce for about 5 minutes.

Add the shrimp back to the pan and swirl in the butter. Heat until the shrimp are warmed through.

To assemble, put some of the shrimp on the bottom half of the puff pastry and spoon over the lemon butter sauce and place the top of the puff pastry over the shrimp. Spoon over more butter sauce.

"The presentation gives not a hint to the simplicity of preparation. Delicious shrimp on a flaky puff pastry with a rich lemon butter sauce will be one of your favorite appetizers."

Continued on page 174.

WINE PAIRING: Gershon Bachus Vintners | Grenache | Flavors of strawberry, raspberry, cranberry with end notes of cinnamon and nutmeg. Delicious chilled.

LEMON BUTTER SAUCE

1 LARGE GARLIC CLOVE, CHOPPED

¼ CUP FRESH LEMON JUICE

1 TSP SALT

½ TSP BLACK PEPPER

½ CUP BUTTER, MELTED

To make the lemon butter sauce, in a blender, purée garlic with lemon juice, salt and pepper until smooth. With the blender running, add melted butter and blend until emulsified, about 30 seconds.

PUFF PASTRY RECTANGLES

1 PKG COMMERCIAL PUFF PASTRY

1 LARGE EGG, LIGHTLY BEATEN WITH 1 TSP WATER

To make the puff pastry rectangles, preheat oven to 400°F.

Cut the puff pastry into rectangles 3 × 3 inches (makes 9) from one sheet of pastry. Place on a baking sheet and paint the top with egg glaze. Wait a minute and paint again with the glaze. Make knife crosshatchings on the top. Bake for 12 to 15 minutes, until pastries are puffed up and brown. While the pastries are hot, split them in half horizontally.

PISSADALIERE (A FRENCH PIZZA)

MAKES 1 (13 × 15 ½ INCH) PISSADALIERE | PREP TIME: 1 ½ HOURS | COOK TIME: 1 HOUR

BASIC DOUGH

- 1 TBSP GRANULATED SUGAR
- 1 CUP WARM WATER (110 TO 115°F)
- 1 ENVELOPE ACTIVE DRY YEAST
- 3 CUPS BREAD OR UNBLEACHED FLOUR
- 1 TSP SALT
- ¼ CUP OLIVE OIL

TOPPING

- ¼ CUP OLIVE OIL
- 6 CUPS (ABOUT 3 LARGE ONIONS), THINLY SLICED
- 2 CLOVES GARLIC, MINCED
- 3 TBSP FRESH THYME LEAVES
- 1 BAY LEAF
- SALT AND PEPPER
- 1 CUP NIÇOISE OR KALAMATA OLIVES, PITTED

To make the dough, lightly oil a 13 × 15 ½ inch baking sheet.

In a small bowl, dissolve sugar in warm water and sprinkle yeast over the top. Stir gently until it dissolves.

Add 3 cups of flour and the salt to a food processor. Pulse to combine. Add yeast mixture and oil and process continuously until the dough forms a single ball on top of the blade, about 30 seconds. Turn out onto a lightly floured surface and knead by hand for about 2 minutes. Place in a well oiled bowl, cover and let rise until doubled, about 1 to 1 ½ hours.

When dough has risen, punch down and pour out onto a lightly floured surface. Roll the dough into a 13 × 15 inch rectangle and place on the prepared baking sheet.

To make the topping, heat olive oil in a sauté pan and add onion, garlic, thyme and bay leaf and cook until the onion is caramelized (45 to 60 minutes). Discard bay leaf and season with salt and pepper.

To assemble, preheat oven to 450°F.

Brush the dough with olive oil, then cover it with the onion sauce. Arrange olives over the onions and drizzle with olive oil. Bake for about 10 minutes. Let cool for 5 minutes and cut into equal squares.

WINE PAIRING: Gershon Bachus Vintners | Petite Syrah | This is a beautiful wine with the aromas and first palete of deep dark fruits—pears, plums, and dates.

LEONESS
CELLARS
2015
TEMECULA VALLEY
SYRAH

LEONESS CELLARS

"THE WORD LEONESS, MEANING 'VILLAGE OF DREAMS', IS THE INSPIRATION BEHIND OUR LIFELONG QUEST TO CREATE WORLD CLASS WINES FROM THE FINEST VINEYARDS IN THE TEMECULA VALLEY."
— Leoness Cellars

Leoness Cellars was founded in 2002 by Mike Rennie and Gary Winder. Together they have over 80 years of agriculture and grape-growing experience in the Temecula Valley and are "dedicated to educating the community about sustainable farming practices." Their combined experience has led to a true understanding of growing wine grapes of the highest quality, grapes which are concentrated, balanced and ripe, ultimately producing wines of incredible depth and flavor.

At Leoness, "they pride themselves on being farmers first" and all the grapes are grown by the estate. The 20 acres of Cabernet Sauvignon was originally planted in 1999 by Stage Ranch. Today, Leoness Cellars sits on a hillside overlooking the original vineyard and "grapes from these vines are used to craft some of the most enjoyable Leoness wines."

In addition to Cabernet Sauvignon, Leoness Cellars produces Syrah, Cabernet Franc, White Merlot, Muscat Canelli, and Cinsault Port. Each of their wines are "carefully crafted to preserve the subtle flavors and nuances of the varietal." Their red wines and chardonnay are aged for an extended time in French or American oak barrels and their white wines are fermented slowly at cool temperatures, "helping the wines retain the fresh fruit flavors of the grape."

Leoness Cellars produces 30,000 cases of wine each year.

CHICKEN ROULADES WITH BLUEBERRY CHUTNEY

SERVES 6 | PREP TIME: 20 MINUTES | COOK TIME: 40 MINUTES

6 (4 TO 6 OZ) BONELESS, SKINLESS CHICKEN BREAST HALVES

1 ⅓ CUP PANKO BREAD CRUMBS

1 TBSP OLIVE OIL

3 EGG WHITES

2 TBSP MILK

2 TSP CORNSTARCH

¼ TSP MUSTARD

1 ½ TSP SALT

¾ TSP BLACK PEPPER

⅓ CUP PROSCIUTTO, FINELY CHOPPED

1 CUP FONTINA CHEESE, SHREDDED

⅔ CUP BLEU CHEESE

3 TBSP FRESH BASIL, FINELY CHOPPED

SPRAY OLIVE OIL

Preheat oven to 350°F.

Pound each chicken breast between plastic wrap to ¼ inch thickness, tapering the edges to ⅛ inch. Set aside.

Drizzle the Panko crumbs with the olive oil and toss until coated.

Heat a large skillet and add the Panko, toasting until golden. Reserve.

In a shallow dish, whisk together the egg whites, milk, cornstarch and mustard.

Set a wire rack over a large baking sheet.

Sprinkle the chicken with salt and pepper.

WINE PAIRING: Leoness Cellars | Mélange d' Ete | A light, crisp and refreshing white wine comprised of five different grape varieties, Viognier, Roussanne, Sauvignon Blanc, Grenache Blanc and Muscat Canelli offering delicious aromas and flavors of peach, pear and grapefruit with a crisp and refreshing taste.

In a small bowl mix the prosciutto, fontina, bleu cheese and chopped basil. Divide the mixture into 6 equal portions. Put a portion of the cheese mixture at the bottom edge (long side) of each breast. Roll the bottom edge of the breast over the filling and roll up tightly, tucking in the sides. Press firmly on the seam to seal.

Roll the chicken roulades in the egg white mixture, then roll in the bread crumbs. Arrange the chicken on the wire rack and spray with olive oil to lightly coat. Bake for about 40 minutes or until the interior of the roulades measures 160°F on an instant thermometer.

Cover the roulades loosely with foil and let rest for 10 minutes. Slice each roulade and fan out on the plate. Serve with blueberry chutney.

Recipe for Blueberry Chutney on page 183.

"THE OWNER OF OUR LOCAL BLUEBERRY FARM ATTENDED MY BLUEBERRY CLASS AND UPON LEAVING ASKED ME IF MY RECIPE WAS PROPRIETARY. I TOLD HIM 'NO' AND NOW THE BLUEBERRY STAND MAKES AND SELLS THIS BLUEBERRY CHUTNEY UNDER THE TEMECULA BERRY FARM LABEL."

BLUEBERRY CHUTNEY

MAKES 2 CUPS | PREP TIME: 10 MINUTES | COOK TIME: 15 MINUTES

- 1 TBSP BUTTER
- ¼ CUP ONION, FINELY CHOPPED
- 3 TBSP WHITE WINE VINEGAR
- ⅓ CUP RAISINS
- 3 TBSP CRYSTALLIZED GINGER
- ⅓ CUP BROWN SUGAR
- ½ TBSP WORCHESTERSHIRE
- ½ TSP CURRY POWDER
- ½ TSP SALT
- ⅛ TSP GROUND NUTMEG
- 1 ½ CUPS BLUEBERRIES, FRESH OR FROZEN

Sauté the onion with the butter until translucent. Stir in the vinegar, raisins, ginger, brown sugar, Worcestershire sauce, curry, salt, nutmeg and blueberries. Bring the mixture to a boil, then reduce the heat to low and simmer for 15 minutes.

Serve at room temperature with the roulades.

Recipe for Chicken Roulades with Blueberry Chutney on page 180.

CHOCOLATE MOUSSE WITH SYRUP OF SYRAH WINE

SERVES 6 | PREP TIME: 15 MINUTES | COOK TIME: 10 MINUTES

SYRAH WINE SYRUP

1 CUP SYRAH WINE (OR OTHER RED WINE)

¼ CUP SUGAR

CHOCOLATE MOUSSE

4 OZ BITTERSWEET CHOCOLATE, FINELY COPPED

6 OZ SEMI-SWEET CHOCOLATE, FINELY CHOPPED

3 TBSP BUTTER, CUT INTO SMALL PIECES

½ CUP SYRAH WINE SYRUP

3 TBSP WATER

1 ½ CUPS HEAVY CREAM

1 TBSP VANILLA EXTRACT

2 TBSP SUGAR

3 EGG YOLKS

GARNISH

WHIPPED CREAM

FRESH RASPBERRIES

To make the syrup, put wine and sugar into a saucepan. Bring to a boil, then reduce to a simmer for 5 minutes. Cool and reserve.

To make the chocolate mousse, put both bittersweet and semi-sweet chocolates, butter, ½ cup of wine syrup and water into a bain-marie (double boiler). Stir the chocolate mixture often until completely melted. Remove from heat and cool slightly.

Whisk the egg yolks into the chocolate mixture until completely blended.

In a seperate bowl, whip the cream with the vanilla and sugar to form soft peaks.

Fold the whipped cream into the chocolate mixture, just until mixed.

Spoon chocolate mousse into small bowls or cups and drizzle remaining syrup over.

Serve with a dollop of whipped cream and fresh raspberries.

"Chocolate and red wine is a heavenly marriage and even more delicious when it's chocolate mousse with a red wine syrup."

WINE PAIRING: Leoness Cellars | Syrah | This syrah is bursting with aromas of black currant, blackberry and boysenberry fruit layered with subtle notes of vanilla, black licorice and sweet oak.

LONGSHADOW RANCH VINEYARD AND WINERY

"BOTTLED WITH PRIDE, THESE WINES ARE A REFLECTION OF OUR HERITAGE." — John and Susan Brodersen, owners, Longshadow Ranch Vineyards and Winery

Longshadow Ranch Vineyard and Winery gives a unique taste of history and charm of the Old West where people are encouraged to "Do one thing every day that makes you happy." Visitors are invited to take carriage rides through the vineyards to see things done the old fashioned way with draft horses and machinery from days gone by. The Belgian draft horses that pull the carriages also work the vineyards. The 26 acres of vineyards planted in 1999 produce eight varietals including Cinsault, Syrah, Tempranillo, Sangiovese, Malbec, Merlot, Cabernet Sauvignon, and Petite Verdot. The names of their wines give a hint of their historic context: Outlaw Red, Wildfire Red and Ponderosa Port.

Longshadow welcomes families to their Saturday evening bonfires. The Brodersens raised their children on the property and enjoy inviting other children to experience country life by interacting with alpacas, sheep and goats.

Longshadow Ranch Vineyard and Winery produce 5,000 cases of wine a year.

LONGSHADOW
RANCH
VINEYARD AND WINERY
Muscat
2017
California
Product of USA

TINY HAM AND SPINACH QUICHES

MAKES 20 TO 24 MINIATURES | PREP TIME: 35 MINUTES | COOK TIME: 20 MINUTES

- 1 RECIPE TART DOUGH (PÂTE BRISÉE)
- 1 ½ TBSP BUTTER
- 2 SHALLOTS, FINELY CHOPPED
- 1 CUP BABY SPINACH, COARSELY CHOPPED
- 2 EGGS
- ⅔ CUP HEAVY CREAM
- ½ TSP DIJON MUSTARD
- ½ TSP SALT
- ¼ TSP PEPPER
- 1 OZ HAM, FINELY DICED
- 2 OZ GRUYÈRE CHEESE, FINELY GRATED

On a floured surface, roll out the tart dough ⅛ inch thick. Using a 2 ½ inch biscuit cutter, cut out as many rounds as you can. Gently put the rounds into the cups of a miniature muffin pan. Refrigerate.

Preheat oven to 400°F.

Sauté the shallots in the butter until softened. Add the spinach and cook until wilted, 1 minute. Remove from heat and reserve.

In a large bowl, whisk together the egg, cream, mustard, salt and pepper. Add the spinach mixture, ham and cheese and stir to combine. Divide the filling among the prepared tart lined mufflin pan.

Bake until the quiches are puffy and golden brown, about 10 to 15 minutes.

Let the quiches cool on a rack for 10 minutes, run a knife around the edges and carefully lift out.

"A pretty addition to a small plates buffet or afternoon tea."

WINE PAIRING: Longshadow Ranch Vineyard and Winery | Cabernet Franc | Full bodied, aged in American Oak with a peppery finish.

TART DOUGH (PÂTE BRISÉE)

2 CUPS ALL PURPOSE FLOUR

12 OZ BUTTER, CUBED

¼ TSP SALT

½ TSP PEPPER

⅓ CUP ICE WATER

Put the flour, salt and butter into a food processor.

Process until the mixture looks like large grains of cornmeal.

With the motor running, add the ice water and process until a ball forms on the blade of the food processor.

Turn out the dough onto a floured surface and divide in half. Shape each piece into a disk about 6 inches in diameter. Wrap in plastic wrap and put into refrigerator for about 30 minutes. Roll out according to recipe.

FRESH GINGER CAKE WITH LEMON SAUCE

SERVES 8 TO 10 | PREP TIME: 10 MINUTES | COOK TIME: 30 MINUTES

- 1 ½ CUPS CAKE FLOUR
- 1 TSP BAKING SODA
- ½ TSP SALT
- 1 LARGE EGG, ROOM TEMPERATURE
- ¼ CUP MOLASSES
- ¼ CUP DARK CORN SYRUP
- ½ CUP WATER
- 4 OZ BUTTER, UNSALTED, ROOM TEMPERATURE
- ½ CUP BROWN SUGAR
- 2 TSP LEMON ZEST
- 2 TSP FRESH GINGER, GRATED
- POWDERED SUGAR FOR DECORATION

Preheat oven to 350°F.

Prepare a 9 inch cake pan by greasing the bottom and sides with butter and dusting with flour. Cut a circular piece of parchment to fit in the bottom.

Put the flour, baking soda and salt into a bowl.

Put the egg into a small bowl and whisk to mix. Put the molasses, corn syrup and water into another bowl and stir to combine.

Place the butter into a bowl of a mixer and cream the butter until it is light and lemony in color. Add the brown sugar and mix until light and fluffy. Add the egg mixture and beat until combined. Stir in the ginger and lemon zest.

Stir ¼ of the flour mixture into the butter mixture. Then add ⅓ of the molasses mixture. Repeat, alternating dry and liquid ingredients ending with flour.

Pour the batter into the cake pan and bake for 30 to 35 minutes. The cake is done when a wooden toothpick inserted into the center of the cake comes out clean.

Put the pan on a cake rack to cool. When cool, dust with powdered sugar. Serve with fresh lemon sauce.

WINE PAIRING: Longshadow Ranch Vineyard and Winery | Muscat of Alexandria | A sweet wine with hints of hibiscus and honey.

LEMON SAUCE

½ CUP SUGAR

1 TBSP CORNSTARCH

1 CUP WATER

3 TBSP BUTTER

½ TSP LEMON ZEST

1 ½ TBSP LEMON JUICE

⅛ TSP SALT

Combine sugar, cornstarch and water in a heat proof bowl. Heat over bain marie (double boiler) until thickened. Remove sauce from heat and stir in butter, lemon zest, lemon juice and salt.

LORENZI ESTATE

DON LORENZI MAKES A WINE LOVER'S WINE.

Don Lorenzi has been making artisan wines from Temecula grapes for about twenty-five years. He has planted the best clones and rootstocks available to match our soil and climate, giving painstaking attention to detail to produce bold, handcrafted, premium wines with a passion. Don knows what he is doing. In the early 1900s two Italian families, the Lorenzis and the De Ambrogios planted Zinfandel vines in the Cucamonga Valley. Don remembers the smell of fermenting grapes at his grandparents' home.

Don also spent time with Philo Biane, a legendary Temecula wine-making pioneer who planted some of the first vines in the valley in 1968. Biane chose to plant in the Temecula Valley knowing the soils of decomposed granite and rich in phosphorus were assets. In 2000, Don's cousin, Steve De Ambrogio, gave him 20 vines cloned from the original 100-year-old vines in Cucamonga and Don started making wine from Pinot Grigio, Cabernet Sauvignon, Merlot and Petite Syrah.

His formula for success is in nurturing the wine from the fruit to the bottle. Lorenzi chose to use a lion for the Lorenzi Estate Winery logo, because it is said that in ancient Rome, Bacchus, the god of wine, used lions to guard his wine caves. The names of his wines are suggestive to the imagination: Catalyst, Obsessive, Alpha Red, Bordello, Brutus, Rated R and Zin City Blend.

What makes a great small lot, handcrafted artisan wine? A wine made by a wine lover. Don Lorenzi makes a wine lover's wine. Don makes 4,000 cases each year.

LORENZI
ESTATE
VINEYARDS AND WINERY
BELLA MIA
BRUT
METHODE CHAMPENOISE

FETTUCCINE WITH WILD MUSHROOMS

SERVES 6 | PREP TIME: 15 MINUTES | COOK TIME: 30 MINUTES

1 TBSP OLIVE OIL

1 ½ OZ PANCETTA, CHOPPED

3 LARGE SHALLOTS, CHOPPED

2 TSP FRESH THYME, MINCED

½ LB WILD MUSHROOMS (SUCH AS SHITAKE OR CREMINI), SLICED

1 CUP CHICKEN BROTH

1 LB DRIED FETTUCCINE OR SPAGHETTI

½ CUP GRATED PARMESAN CHEESE

Sauté the pancetta until crispy and set aside. Add the shallots and thyme to the pan and sauté until the shallots are lightly browned. Add the mushrooms and season with salt and pepper and sauté until tender. Add the crispy pancetta to the mushroom mixture.

Add the broth and simmer until lightly thickened.

While the mushroom mixture is simmering, bring a large pot of salted water to a boil. Add the pasta and cook until al dente, about 8 minutes.

Drain the pasta and add to the mushroom mixture. Toss until the pasta is coated with the mushroom mixture. Stir in the cheese and taste for salt and pepper.

"I was privileged to forage for mushrooms in Colorado with an expert and this is the preparation I chose for those treasured mushrooms. If you can find morels, they are the best."

WINE PAIRING: Lorenzi Estate | Syrah | An earthy and hardy wine with a full tannic finish.

ROASTED SALMON WITH WILD MUSHROOMS AND KALE

SERVES 6 | PREP TIME: 10 MINUTES | COOK TIME: 40 MINUTES

1 BUNCH KALE LEAVES IN BITE-SIZED PIECES

⅓ CUP OLIVE OIL

1 LB WILD MUSHROOMS (SHITAKE, PORCINI, CREMINI OR A COMBINATION), STEMS REMOVED AND CUT INTO 1 INCH PIECES

4 CLOVES GARLIC, MINCED

½ TSP BALSAMIC VINEGAR

1 ½ LBS SALMON FILETS, CUT INTO 4 OZ PORTIONS

SALT AND PEPPER

Preheat oven to 375°F.

Oil a baking sheet. Drizzle the kale with olive oil and sprinkle with salt. Toss to mix and scatter the kale on the oiled baking sheet.

Bake for 15 minutes. Remove from oven and reserve.

Put another baking sheet in the oven to warm.

Heat 3 tablespoons of the olive oil in a sauté pan and cook the mushrooms until all the liquid from the mushrooms has evaporated. Season with salt and pepper and stir in the garlic and vinegar. Set aside and keep warm.

Season the salmon filets with salt and pepper and put them on the warmed baking sheet.

Bake for 10 minutes.

Divide the salmon among plates and top with the mushrooms and garnish with the kale.

"Salmon is a useful ingredient. It can be baked, poached, grilled, sautéed and cooked in a paper bag. I like this updated version which incorporates mushrooms and kale."

WINE PAIRING: Lorenzi Estate | Pinot Noir | This is a classic wine with aromas of black cherries, dried figs and rose hips.

OEUFS

SERVES 6 | PREP TIME: 20 MINUTES | COOK TIME: 30 MINUTES

SAUCE

5 TBSP BUTTER, UNSALTED

2 TBSP ONION OR SHALLOTS, FINELY CHOPPED

3 TBSP WATER

6 TBSP ALL PURPOSE FLOUR

1 CUP CHICKEN BROTH

1 CUP MILK

1 CUP HEAVY CREAM

2 OZ SWISS OR GRUYÈRE CHEESE, GRATED

SALT AND PEPPER TO TASTE

OEUFS

6 EGGS, HARD BOILED

¼ CUP PARSLEY, MINCED

2 CLOVES GARLIC, MINCED

¼ CUP HEAVY CREAM

½ TSP SALT

¼ TSP PEPPER

Preheat the oven to 350°F.

For the sauce, melt the butter in a saucepan, add the onion and water and cook over moderate heat for about 2 minutes, until the water is evaporated. Stir in the flour and cook on low heat whipping constantly with a wire whisk for 3 minutes. Add the chicken broth and bring to a boil. Add the milk and bring to a boil again. Reduce the heat and simmer for 5 minutes. Stir in the cream and bring to a boil again. Season to taste.

While the sauce is cooking, cut the hard boiled eggs in half and place the yolks into a seperate bowl. Mash the yolks with a fork until smooth. Mix in the parsley, garlic, heavy cream, and salt and pepper. Fill each egg half with the yolk mixture.

Place the egg halves in a buttered baking dish or individual ramekins with the yolks facing up and pour the sauce over. Sprinkle with cheese. Bake for 10 to 15 minutes until the cheese is melted and the eggs are heated through.

"I've been serving this breakfast or brunch dish to my family for decades and it is our Christmas morning tradition. It's a handy dish because it can be prepped the day before, refrigerated and baked when ready to serve."

WINE PAIRING: Lorenzi Estate | Bella Mia Brut | A crisp sparkling wine with flavors of green apple and pear.

LORIMAR VINEYARDS AND WINERY

HANDCRAFTED WINES WITH A FRUIT FORWARD STYLE SHOWCASE CLEAN CRISP FRUIT.

Brothers-in-law Lawrie Lipton and Mark Manfield had a dream and saw it to fruition with the opening of Lorimar Vineyards and Winery. The name Lorimar is a merge of their names Lawrie and Mark. In 2009 they opened a tasting bar in Old Town Temecula and in 2012 they opened Lorimar Winery, a Tuscan-style winery in the Temecula Valley Wine Country.

The handcrafted wines with a fruit forward style showcase clean crisp fruit. "Our winemaker creates wines using the best of the Old World ways combined with today's more advanced technology, producing delicious varietals and interesting blends."

Lorimar Winery's distinct personality is built upon a fusion of wine, art, music and food in an "inspiring escape of the senses." They offer reds, whites, blushes, and sparkling dessert wines and bottle 12,000 to 13,000 cases each year.

We suggest putting on some cool jazz or passionate classical music while you enjoy Lorimar wines.

CALIFORNIA
2018
WHITE
MERLOT
Lorimar
VINEYARDS AND WINERY

CHICKEN LETTUCE WRAPS

SERVES 6 | PREP TIME: 15 MINUTES | COOK TIME: 35 MINUTES

2 ½ TSP SOY SAUCE

2 TBSP BROWN SUGAR

1 ½ TSP DARK SESAME OIL

1 TBSP WHITE/YELLOW MISO PASTE
+ HOT SAUCE (OPTIONAL)

1 TBSP GARLIC, MINCED

¼ TSP PEPPER

1 LB BONELESS, SKINLESS CHICKEN BREASTS, THINLY SLICED

1 CUP COOKED RICE

2 TSP VEGETABLE OIL

1 TSP SESAME SEEDS, TOASTED (OPTIONAL)

12 BIBB LETTUCE LEAVES

24 CUCUMBER SLICES

4 GREEN ONIONS, FINELY SLICED

Make the marinade by combining the soy sauce, brown sugar, sesame oil, miso, garlic and pepper in a large resealable plastic bag. Add chicken slices to bag and refrigerate for 30 minutes.

Remove chicken slices from bag and discard marinade. Heat a skillet and add the vegetable oil to the pan. Add the drained chicken and sauté for 2 minutes on each side or until cooked through.

Warm the cooked rice.

Sprinkle sesame seeds over the chicken. Take one lettuce leaf, layer 2 tablespoons of rice on the leaf and add a generous amount of chicken. Add a few cucumber slices and a sprinkling of green onions.

"This is a simple and flavorful dish for lunch or a summer supper. For a heartier meal you can add Cold Avocado Soup with Fresh Crab (recipe on page 222) or a Spring Pasta Salad (recipe on page 219)."

WINE PAIRING: Lorimar Vineyards and Winery | White Merlot | Aromas and flavors of red berries with a sweet finish.

GRILLED ROSEMARY SHRIMP

SERVES 6 | PREP TIME: 30 MINUTES | COOK TIME: 10 MINUTES

6 ROSEMARY BRANCHES

18 LARGE SHRIMP, SHELLED AND DEVEINED

OLIVE OIL

SALT AND PEPPER

ARUGULA FOR SERVING

CANTALOUPE SALSA

3 TBSP OLIVE OIL

1 TBSP FRESH LEMON JUICE

1 SMALL SHALLOT, MINCED

1 TBSP FRESH GINGER, MINCED

1 MEDIUM CANTALOUPE, PEELED, SEEDED AND DICED

2 CUCUMBERS PEELED, SEEDED AND DICED

1 TBSP CILANTRO, CHOPPED

Strip off most of the leaves on the rosemary branches leaving 2 to 3 inches of leaves at the top.

Place the rosemary branches in a shallow pan of water to soak for 20 minutes. This will keep the skewers from burning.

Skewer 3 shrimp on each rosemary skewer, brush with olive oil, season with salt and grill for 3 minutes on each side.

To make the salsa, in a medium bowl, stir the olive oil with the lemon juice, shallot, ginger and cilantro. Mix in the cantaloupe and cucumber and season with salt.

To serve, place a mound of arugula on each plate and place a shrimp skewer on top. Top with the cucumber salsa and drizzle with olive oil.

"Rosemary branches act as skewers for grilling and impart an herby minty flavor to the shrimp. The skewers with rosemary leaves left on the top look very festive."

WINE PAIRING: Lorimar Vineyards and Winery | Viognier | Off dry with tropical fruit and flavors of peaches and pears.

LUMIERE WINERY

"LUMIERE WINERY IS A LABOR OF LOVE AND A LOVE OF NATURE."
— Lumiere Winery

The Lumiere vineyard was originally planted with Sauvignon Blanc by the Barlin family in the 1980s. In 1987 Dr. Ezra Kleiner and his wife Martha purchased the property. Ezra, Martha and their two children came from Los Angeles every weekend to tend the grapes in what Dr. Kleiner lovingly named Martha's Vineyard. They sold their harvests to various wineries until the early 2000s. When young Andrew Kleiner grew up, he studied viticulture and enology at UC Davis to prepare him for his role as Lumiere's vineyard manager and winemaker.

Andrew is convinced that good wine begins in the vineyard with good grapes and he is pleased with what he calls, "the amazing fruit produced in the Lumiere vineyard." He has grafted in Merlot, Cabernet Franc, Cabernet Sauvignon, and Petite Verdot, major Bordeaux varietals, while continuing to produce from the original Sauvignon Blanc vines.

The winery's name Lumiere means "light" in French. For the Kleiner family, the name represents "the source of life and happiness." In order for grapes to come to fruition, plants must have sunlight. The Kleiners joyously lift a glass to toast light, life, and happiness. They encourage everyone to "share the light." Lumiere Winery produces 1,000 to 1,500 cases of wine a year.

Lumière
Winery
Sauvignon Blanc
"FASHIONABLY LATE"
ESTATE BOTTLED
2017

LEEK AND POTATO GALETTE

SERVES 4 TO 8 | PREP TIME: 20 MINUTES | COOK TIME: 50 MINUTES

CRUST

½ CUP UNSALTED PISTACHIOS, SHELLED

2 ½ CUPS FLOUR

1 TSP SALT

1 TSP SUGAR

8 OZ BUTTER, CHILLED AND CUT INTO ¼ INCH DICE

⅓ CUP ICE WATER

Continued on page 220

To make the crust, pulse pistachios in a food processor until ground coarsely. Add flour, salt and sugar and pulse. Add butter and pulse until it resembles coarse cornmeal.

Slowly add water and process until dough forms a ball on the blade of the processor. Form into a disk, wrap in plastic wrap and chill.

Continued on page 212.

WINE PAIRING: Lumiere Winery | Sauvignon Blanc | Delightful hints of apple with sweet cherry notes that mingle with fresh flavors of raspberries which lead up to a deliciously crisp finish.

FILLING

1 TBSP OLIVE OIL

1 LARGE LEEK, HALVED LENGTHWISE AND THINLY SLICED HORIZONTALLY

5 OZ GOAT CHEESE, AT ROOM TEMPERATURE

5 TBSP HEAVY CREAM

2 CLOVES GARLIC, MINCED

SALT AND PEPPER

4 TBSP FRESH DILL, MINCED

2 LARGE YUKON GOLD POTATOES, THINLY SLICED

1 LG EGG, LIGHTLY BEATEN

FRESH DILL SPRIGS FOR GARNISH

Preheat oven to 400°F.

To make the filling, cook leek in 1 tbsp oil until translucent, not browned, about 5 minutes. Set aside.

In a bowl, mix goat cheese, cream and garlic and season with salt and pepper to taste. Set aside.

Divide dough into four pieces. Roll out 1 piece of dough to an 8 inch round and transfer to a parchment lined baking sheet. Repeat with the other three pieces.

Spread goat cheese mixture over the dough, leaving a 1 inch border. Arrange one layer of potatoes over the goat cheese and sprinkle the leeks over the potatoes.

Scatter 1 tbsp of the dill over the leeks and top with another thin layer of potato slices. Drizzle with oil.

Fold edges of dough over filling. Repeat with remaining dough to make a total of four galettes.

Brush top of the galette with the lightly beaten egg.

Bake galettes until crusts are golden brown and potatoes are soft, 30 to 40 minutes. Drizzle with olive oil and top with dill sprigs.

"THIS HAS BECOME
A FAVORITE IN MY
HOUSEHOLD. A FLAKY
CRUST AND THE UNUSUAL
ADDITION OF PISTACHIOS
MAKES IT SPECIAL FOR
HOME MEALS AND A
NICE ADDITION TO YOUR
APPETIZER REPERTOIRE."

SALMON STRUDEL

SERVES 6 | PREP TIME: 30 MINUTES + 6 HOURS FOR MARINADE | COOK TIME: 10 MINUTES

MARINADE

12 OZ SALMON, CUT INTO 2 OZ PORTIONS

½ CUP OLIVE OIL

1 ORANGE, ZEST ONLY

1 LEMON, ZEST ONLY

1 TBSP CHOPPED DILL

ASSEMBLE AND COOK

6 GRAPE LEAVES (IN A JAR)

6 SHEETS FILO DOUGH

½ CUP BUTTER, MELTED

To make the marinade, mix olive oil, dill and zests together. Marinate salmon pieces for 6 hours.

Preheat oven to 450°F.

To make the strudel, carefully remove the grape leaves from the jar and spread on paper towels to drain.

Wrap each piece of fish tightly in a grape leaf. Lay out 1 piece of the filo and butter lightly with pastry brush.

Place fish at a long end of the filo and fold outer edges over the salmon. Begin rolling the salmon in the filo, buttering between each roll.

Brush tops of salmon strudels with remaining butter.

Bake until golden brown, about 6 to 8 minutes.

"I've tried this recipe with blanched fresh grape leaves but the canned ones are better."

WINE PAIRING: Lumiere Winery | Cabernet Sauvignon | A full bodied red wine with notes of black cherry and black olive.

PUMPKIN FLAN

MAKES 1 (10 INCH) FLAN OR 8 RAMEKINS | PREP TIME: 30 MINUTES | COOK TIME: 45 MINUTES

- 1 CUP SUGAR, FOR COATING RAMEKINS
- ½ CUP WATER
- 6 WHOLE EGGS
- 6 EGG YOLKS
- 2 CUPS HALF AND HALF
- 1 TSP VANILLA
- 1 TSP CINNAMON
- 1 CUP SWEETENED CONDENSED MILK
- 7 OZ CANNED PUMPKIN PIE FILLING
- PINCH OF SALT
- PINE NUT BRITTLE FOR GARNISH

Preheat oven to 350°F.

Melt the sugar and water in a saucepan over medium-high heat. Cook and swirl the pan until the sugar is lightly browned. Use a brush with cold water to wash down any crystals that form on the edge of the pan. Pour enough of the caramelized sugar into each ramekin to coat the bottom. While the caramelized sugar is still hot and liquid, swirl each ramekin to coat the sides. Set ramekins aside to cool.

In a bowl, whisk together the eggs, egg yolks, half and half, vanilla, cinnamon, condensed milk, pumpkin pie filling and salt. Pour into the prepared ramekins.

Place the ramekins in a baking pan and fill the pan with 1 inch of hot water. Place the pan in the oven. Bake for about 45 minutes or until the custard is set in the middle. Remove ramekins from the pan, let cool and refrigerate for 4 hours.

To serve, unmold the ramekins over a serving plate, pulling at the sides with your fingers to break the vacuum in the ramekin. If you need to, a knife can be run around the edge.

Top with pine nut brittle.

WINE PAIRING: Lumiere Winery | Late Harvest Sauvignon Blanc | A rich, luscious wine with intense aromas and flavors of peach, dried fig, pineapple and honey with an excellent balance.

PINE NUT BRITTLE

1 ½ CUPS SUGAR

½ CUP LIGHT CORN SYRUP

¾ CUP PINE NUTS

To make the pine nut brittle, coat a 12 × 17 inch rimmed baking sheet with cooking spray.

Bring sugar and corn syrup to a boil in a medium saucepan, stirring and brushing down sides with a wet pastry brush to prevent sugar crystals from forming, until sugar dissolves. Cook, swirling occasionally until mixture starts to turn golden around edges.

Stir in the pine nuts. Cook, stirring occasionally, until mixture is pale amber, about 5 to 8 minutes. Pour onto baking sheet without spreading, moving the sheet around until the mixture flows over it forming a thin layer. Let cool. Break pine nut brittle into pieces.

SPRING PASTA SALAD

SERVES 6 | PREP TIME: 20 MINUTES | COOK TIME: 10 MINUTES

- 1 ½ CUPS ORZO PASTA
- 6 OZ GREEN BEANS, CUT INTO 2 INCH PIECES AND BLANCHED
- 12 CHERRY TOMATOES, HALVED
- 2 CARROTS, CUT INTO ½ INCH DICE
- 1 CUP PARSLEY, CHOPPED
- 3 TBSP CAPERS, DRAINED
- ¼ CUP OLIVE OIL
- 1 TBSP FRESH MINT, CHOPPED
- JUICE OF 1 LEMON
- SALT AND PEPPER

Bring a pot of water to boil and add 1 tbsp salt. Add pasta and cook until done, about 8 to 9 minutes. Pour pasta into a strainer and immediately run cold water over the pasta to stop the cooking.

In a bowl, mix together pasta, green beans, cherry tomatoes, carrots, parsley, capers and mint.

Toss with olive oil and lemon juice. Season with salt and pepper to taste.

Serve at room temperature.

"This colorful and fresh salad makes a good accompaniment for spring and summer grills. It keeps well and is a good picnic choice."

MAURICE CAR'RIE VINEYARD AND WINERY

"THE OLDER THE VINE, THE BETTER THE WINE."
— Maurice Car'rie Vineyard and Winery

In 1984 Budd and Maurice Van Roekel bought 46 acres of Temecula Valley's first commercial vineyard, the one planted in 1968 by Vincenzo Cilurzo on land where the Vail Cattle Company had an outpost called Yoder Camp. There, next to the Vail barn, windmill, and water tank Vincenzo planted Chenin Blanc.

Budd and Maurice owned several successful roller skating rinks in Orange County when they decided to retire in the quiet and remote Temecula Valley to relax and enjoy their golden years. Budd thought he might become a "gentleman farmer" riding a tractor with a few dogs and chickens running around.

What they found in Temecula was a huge opportunity and instead of relaxation, Budd began to build the Maurice Car'rie Vineyard and Winery, one of the largest, most flourishing wineries in Temecula. Budd and Maurice worked diligently toward their goal to produce the highest quality wines possible at the most affordable prices possible.

In 2019 the Van Roekels sold the winery to Janak Patel. The heritage of the Cilurzos and the Van Roekels continue to inspire the staff. The Cilurzo vineyard is remembered by the logo of the historical white barn and windmill on the Maurice Car'rie label.

Maurice Car'rie Vineyard and Winery is best known for their white wines ranging from an award-winning dry Sauvignon Blanc to a Platinum award winning Gewürztraminer. Their two distinctive labels distinguish the styles of wine. The Maurice Car'rie Vineyard and Winery label marks the sweeter white, blush, and red wines. The Van Roekel Estate label identifies the dry whites and bold reds. Between the two labels they produce 17,000 cases a year, of over 27 types of wine of 12 whites, 6 sparkling, 10 reds, and a Cream Sherry. Their 2005 Port was voted the Best Wine in Southern California in 2016 by the American Wine Society.

Maurice Car'rie
WINERY
Celebrating
30
YEARS
CHENIN BLANC "SOFT"
ESTATE GROWN
Vintage 2017
TEMECULA VALLEY

COLD AVOCADO SOUP WITH FRESH CRAB

SERVES 6 TO 10 | PREP TIME: 15 MINUTES

- 4 RIPE AVOCADOS, PEELED, SEEDED AND SLICED
- 2 CUPS HEAVY CREAM
- 2 CUPS SOUR CREAM
- 2 SHALLOTS, PEELED
- 2 GREEN ONIONS, CHOPPED
- 1 CUP CHICKEN STOCK
- 1 TSP SALT
- ½ TSP TABASCO SAUCE
- JUICE OF 1 LEMON
- ½ TSP GROUND CUMIN
- 8 OZ FRESH CRAB FOR GARNISH

In two batches, blend all the ingredients, except the crab. Chill until ready to serve. Put into small cups or bowls and garnish with crab.

"A rich and flavorful cold soup meant especially for summer dining. I grew up in the avocado business and my husband and I owned a commercial avocado ranch. Dishes made with avocados always seem luxurious to me. When I was vacationing in Martinique we were served a chilled avocado half with a simple vinaigrette and it was scrumptious."

WINE PAIRING: Maurice Car'rie Vineyard and Winery | Zinfandel Rosé | Floral and berry notes. Citrus flavors lend a bright acidity.

CARAMELIZED APPLE AND ONION TART

MAKES 32 TARTS | PREP TIME: 15 MINUTES | COOK TIME: 1 HOUR 5 MINUTES

2 TBSP OLIVE OIL

1 ½ LB YELLOW ONIONS, THINLY SLICED

1 TSP SALT

2 TBSP BUTTER

1 LB APPLES, PEELED AND SLICED ⅛ INCH THICK

1 TBSP SUGAR

2 OZ GRUYÈRE CHEESE, COARSELY GRATED

2 TBSP CHIVES, MINCED

1 TSP FRESH THYME, CHOPPED

¼ TSP BLACK PEPPER

1 LB FROZEN PUFF PASTRY DOUGH

1 EGG, BEATEN WITH 2 TBSP WATER

Add the olive oil to a sauté pan, heat and add the onions and the salt. Cook about 30 minutes until the onions are brown and caramelized. Put into a bowl to cool.

Melt the butter in a sauté pan and add the apples and sugar and cook until the apples have softened, about 10 minutes. Transfer to the bowl with the onions and add cheese, chives, thyme and pepper. Let cool to room temperature.

Preheat oven to 400°F.

Line two baking sheets with parchment.

Put the puff pastry on a work space and cut into 2 inch squares. Place pastry squares on the baking sheets.

Brush the pastry squares with the egg wash and place a heaping 1 tbsp of the onion and apple mixture in the center of each square.

Bake until the pastry is crisp on the bottom and browned on the top, about 25 minutes.

Let the tarts cool to room temperature.

"This appetizer has sweet and savory flavors and a satisfying buttery taste. It's very easy to make and draws raves on a buffet table or small plates menu."

WINE PAIRING: Maurice Car'rie Vineyard and Winery | Chenin Blanc | Floral aromas with flavors of melon, honeydew and pear. A slightly sweet finish.

BRAISED CHICKEN WITH MUSHROOMS

SERVES 6 TO 8 | PREP TIME: 15 MINUTES | COOK TIME: 1 HOUR 15 MINUTES

6 TBSP OLIVE OIL

3 GARLIC CLOVES, CHOPPED

1 (4 LB) CHICKEN, CUT INTO SERVING PIECES

1 CUP DRY WHITE WINE

SALT AND PEPPER

1 ¼ LB MUSHROOMS (SHITAKE, CREMINI, BUTTON OR A MIXTURE)

1 TBSP FRESH THYME LEAVES

In a heavy pan over low heat, warm 3 tbsp of olive oil. Add the garlic and fry gently until translucent, about 3 minutes. Salt and pepper the chicken pieces and brown until golden, about 10 minutes. Add the wine, cover and cook over low heat until tender, about 1 hour or until an instant thermometer reads 160 to 165°F. This dish can also be cooked in a 350°F oven for 1 hour. Always check the level of the liquid and add a little more wine or some chicken stock if it seems dry.

When the chicken is almost done cooking, trim the stems from the mushrooms and slice the mushroom caps. In a separate skillet over moderate heat, warm the remaining 3 tbsp of olive oil. Add the mushrooms and thyme and cook for about 3 minutes.

Add the mushrooms to the pan with the chicken and serve.

"My grandmother called this, 'a Sunday supper dish.' It can be made the day before, refrigerated and reheated." Pair with Rice with Pine Nuts and Peas, recipe on page 229.

WINE PAIRING: Maurice Car'rie Vineyard and Winery | Sauvignon Blanc | A fresh and inviting wine with bright citrus fruits and tropical notes. Flavors of grapefruit, passion fruit and guava.

RICE WITH PINE NUTS AND PEAS

SERVES 8 | PREP TIME: 10 MINUTES | COOK TIME: 30 MINUTES

- 1 CUP LONG GRAIN RICE
- 2 CUPS CHICKEN STOCK
- 1 TBSP BUTTER
- 1TBSP OLIVE OIL
- ½ CUP ONIONS, DICED
- ¼ CUP PINE NUTS
- 1 TSP LEMON ZEST, GRATED
- ½ TSP SALT
- ½ CUP FROZEN PEAS, DO NOT DEFROST

Put the rice and chicken stock in a saucepan and bring to a boil.

Cover, reduce the heat to low and cook for 18 to 20 minutes.

Heat the butter and oil in a sauté pan and add the onion. Cook until the onion is translucent, then add the pine nuts. Cook for 5 minutes stirring until the nuts are browned.

Add the rice, lemon zest and salt to the pan with the onions and pine nuts. Add the peas and cook for 2 minutes longer.

Serve hot.

"This makes a perfect side dish to the Braised Chicken with Mushrooms (recipe on page 226) or the Cornish Game Hens with Prosciutto and Sage (recipe on page 274). The peas and lemon zest are pretty sticking up out of the rice, making it a colorful accompaniment."

ALMOND CAKE WITH FRESH STRAWBERRY SAUCE

SERVES 6 | PREP TIME: 20 MINUTES | COOK TIME: 25 MINUTES

7 OZ ALMOND PASTE

¼ CUP SUGAR

8 TBSP BUTTER, CUT INTO SMALL PIECES AND CHILLED

2 TBSP HONEY

3 LARGE EGGS, ROOM TEMPERATURE

2 TBSP MAURICE CAR'RIE VINEYARD AND WINERY, CANELLI

⅓ CUP ALL PURPOSE FLOUR

PINCH OF SALT

½ CUP SLICED ALMONDS, TOASTED

POWDERED SUGAR

FRESH STRAWBERRY SAUCE

¾ CUP CRÈME FRAÎCHE, WHIPPED INTO SOFT PEAKS

Preheat oven to 350°F.

Butter and flour an 8 inch cake pan and line the bottom with parchment.

Place the almond paste and sugar in the bowl of a mixer fitted with the paddle attachment. Cream the mixture on low speed to break up the almond paste, then increase the speed to medium for about 2 minutes. Add the butter and mix until the mixture is light in color, about 4 to 5 minutes. Mix in the honey, then add the eggs one at a time. Add the Angelica, flour, a pinch of salt and mix to combine.

Pour the batter into the cake pan and bake for about 25 minutes, until the cake is golden and springs back when pressed. Cool on a rack.

Unmold the cake and brush the top of the cake with Canelli wine and sprinkle with the toasted almonds. Dust with powdered sugar.

Serve with a dollop of crème fraîche and fresh strawberry sauce.

WINE PAIRING: Maurice Car'rie Vineyard and Winery | Canelli | A clean and crisp dessert wine with flavors of peaches, apricots and ripe melon. Finishg taste of citrus.

FRESH STRAWBERRY SAUCE

2 LB STRAWBERRIES, RINSED, HULLED AND CUT INTO QUARTERS

¾ CUP SUGAR

Add 1 ½ lb of the strawberries to a bowl. Add the sugar and mash with a potato masher. Let macerate for 1 hour. Add in the ½ lb of quartered strawberries and stir to combine.

Refrigerate.

"A simple cake with fresh strawberries is a perfect summer dessert.

MIRAMONTE WINERY

"A FEW OF US ARE WORKING HARD TO CONSISTENTLY PRODUCE WINES WHICH ARE CLEARLY REDEFINING SOUTHERN CALIFORNIA WINEMAKING." — Cane Vanderhoof, owner, Miramonte Winery

Miramonte was one of the first wineries in the Temecula Valley, originally owned by John Piconi, M.D. When Cane Vanderhoof bought Miramonte in 2001 he was one of the first to focus on Rhone grapes varieties of Syrah, Grenache, Mourvedre and Cinsault.

In 2005, a few close friends, all avid wine collectors and enthusiasts, joined the winery ownership. The group's natural synergy, and its passion for premium wines have kept Miramonte at the forefront of Temecula Valley winemaking. "It's because we're a bunch of wine geeks," says Vanderhoof.

"We chose Temecula over the North and Central coasts," says Vanderhoof, "because we believe it's where Napa was 30 years ago. A few of us are working hard to consistently produce wines which are clearly redefining Southern California winemaking. The transformation is taking place this instant, right before our eyes. We're excited to be one of the wineries leading the effort."

Miramonte has emerged as one of the most respected and heavily awarded wineries of Southern California. Since 2008, they've planted traditional Spanish and Portuguese varieties like Tempranillo, Touriga Nacional, Albariño and Verdelho, which grow extremely well in Temecula, and some lesser known varieties: Macabeo/Viura, Torrontes, Xarello, and the northern Italian Teroldego.

Miramonte works closely with vineyard management practices to grow grapes with consistent concentration, depth of character, and intensity, year-after-year. Each vine is carefully managed, yields are extremely limited and farmed for a careful sense of balance to capture the purest Southern California expression of each variety. Miramonte produces 5,000 cases each year.

MIRAMONTE WINERY
Moscato
2018

CORN AND POBLANO CHILE SOUP

SERVES 6 | PREP TIME: 15 MINUTES | COOK TIME: 20 MINUTES

3 TBSP POBLANO CHILE, DICED

6 TBSP QUESO FRESCO, CRUMBLED

6 SMALL TORTILLAS, CUT INTO SMALL SQUARES AND FRIED CRISP

4 CUPS FRESH CORN (ABOUT 5 EARS)

2 CUPS CREAM

¼ CUP BUTTER

2 ½ CUPS HALF AND HALF

½ TSP SALT

Blend the corn with 1 cup of cream until you have a smooth purée.

In a pot, melt the butter and add the corn purée. Let it cook over a medium flame for about 5 minutes, stirring constantly.

Add the remaining cream, half and half and salt to the mixture and bring it to a boil. Lower the heat and let the soup simmer for about 15 minutes, stirring it from time to time so that it does not stick to the pot.

Put about ½ tbsp of the diced poblano chile and 1 tbsp of crumbled queso fresco into each bowl. Pour over the hot soup and garnish with the tortilla squares.

NOTE: This soup will freeze well.

WINE PAIRING: Miramonte Winery | Tempranillo | Bold, dusty tannins and a long satiny finish showcase endless dark berry and chocolate notes.

BLUEBERRY SALAD WITH PROSCIUTTO AND MELON

SERVES 6 AS AN ENTRÉE OR 12 SMALL SIDES | PREP TIME: 15 MINUTES

- 2 TBSP OLIVE OIL
- 2 TBSP FRESH LIME JUICE
- 2 TBSP PARSLEY, CHOPPED
- ½ TSP SALT
- ¼ TSP LIME ZEST
- 2 TBSP SUGAR
- 2 CUPS FRESH BLUEBERRIES
- 1 SMALL FENNEL BULB, TRIMMED, HALVED VERTICALLY, CORED AND CUT HORIZONTALLY INTO ¼ INCH WIDE STRIPS
- ½ CUP RED ONION, THINLY SLICED
- 12 SLICES PROSCIUTTO
- 12 WEDGES OF CANTALOUPE, PEELED AND CUT ¼ INCH THICK

Mix olive oil, lime juice, parsley, lime zest, sugar and salt together. Stir in blueberries, fennel and onion.

Put a slice of prosciutto on a plate and top with melon. Spoon blueberry mixture over the top and serve immediately.

"This salad was an item on my cooking class blueberry menu. The combination of fruit, meat and fennel make a tasty and colorful plate and can be used as an entrée or a side dish."

WINE PAIRING: Miramonte Winery | Pinot Gris | Flavors of golden apple, ripe nectarine, pineapple and lemon grass with a crisp finish.

MONTE DE ORO WINERY

"WHERE OLD WORLD CHARM MEETS NEW WORLD SOPHISTICATION."
— Monte De Oro Winery

Monte De Oro is one of Temecula Valley's newest Wineries with a passion for growing quality estate grapes and handcrafting premier wines. Monte De Oro's 100% estate grown, award winning wines start in the winery's 72 vineyard acres where great care is taken to cultivate quality grapes from the time they bud in the spring to the time they are harvested in the fall. Annual grape production is between 125 and 180 tons generating between 8,000 and 11,000 cases of wine.

The Monte De Oro Winery came about in 2002 when a collection of 107 owners from America, South Africa and the United Kingdom combined their passion for wine with their collected business experiences to form One Great Blend (OGB) Partners.

They say their winery is where "Old World Charm meets New World Sophistication." Monte de Oro wines are fruit-forward, elegant, balanced and well-structured. Since opening in Temecula in 2010, Monte de Oro has won more than 35 awards and scored many 90+ Point scores for their wines.

MONTE DE ORO
ESTATE GROWN
NOSTIMO
2017
WHITE WINE
TEMECULA VALLEY
CALIFORNIA

KOMATSU

STUFFED FLANK STEAK

SERVES 8 | PREP TIME: 40 MINUTES | COOK TIME: 1 HOUR 45 MINUTES

2 ½ TO 3 LB FLANK STEAK, TRIMMED

STUFFING

- ¼ CUP OLIVE OIL
- 3 TBSP BUTTER
- 2 ½ CUPS BREAD CUBES, MADE WITH WHITE BREAD, ABOUT 1 INCH SQUARE
- 1 LB LEAN GROUND BEEF
- 2 EGGS
- 1 MEDIUM ONION, PEELED AND CHOPPED
- ½ RIB CELERY, PEELED AND FINELY CHOPPED
- 2 TBSP PARSLEY, CHOPPED
- 1 ½ TSP SALT
- ¼ TSP PEPPER

Press the flank steak flat with one hand and cut into the steak lengthwise to make a pocket for the stuffing. Keep the blade horizontal, being careful not to cut all the way through.

To make the stuffing, heat the oil and butter in a skillet and brown the bread cubes.

Combine the remaining ingredients in a large bowl and add the bread cubes, mixing lightly, do not crush.

Stuff the steak. Bring the lower lip of the flank against the stuffing. Bring the upper lip down on top and tuck under for a nice loaf. Tie the roast with kitchen string.

WINE PAIRING: Monte De Oro Winery | Cabernet Sauvignon | Balanced acidity and alcohol with clean and youthful red fruits on the nose with hints of spice. Flavors of black cherry, plum and craisins with brown sugar, black pepper and fennel rounding out the taste.

BRAISING THE FLANK STEAK

1 TBSP BUTTER

1 TBSP OLIVE OIL

1 MEDIUM CARROT, PEELED AND FINELY DICED

1 MEDIUM ONION, CHOPPED

2 BAY LEAVES

1 TOMATO, COARSELY CHOPPED

1 TSP THYME LEAVES

1 CUP BEEF STOCK

1 CUP DRY RED WINE

2 TBSP ARROWROOT

¼ CUP COLD WATER

SALT AND PEPPER

Preheat oven to 350°F.

To braise the flank steak, heat the butter and oil in a deep heavy casserole dish. Brown the stuffed steak on all sides. Add carrot, onion, bay leaves, tomato and thyme and cook over moderate heat for 5 minutes. Add beef stock and wine, bring to a boil, cover and braise in a 350°F oven for 1 ½ hours. When done, remove the stuffed steak to a platter and keep warm while you make the sauce.

To make the sauce, skim the fat from the surface of the braising liquid. Mix the arrowroot and cold water and stir into the liquid. Bring to a boil, stirring constantly, until sauce begins to thicken. Season with salt and pepper.

Cut the meat in ½ inch slices and pour 2 or 3 tbsp of the sauce over each serving.

"Braising is my favorite way to cook any meat. The long slow cooking in a liquid results in moist, deep flavors."

GRITS SOUFFLÉ

SERVES 6 | PREP TIME: 20 MINUTES | COOK TIME: 30 MINUTES

- 2 CUPS MILK
- ½ CUP QUICK GRITS
- ½ TSP SALT
- ½ TSP BAKING POWDER
- 2 TBSP BUTTER, MELTED
- ½ TSP SUGAR
- 1 CUP CHEDDAR CHEESE
- 3 LARGE EGGS, SEPARATED

Preheat oven to 375°F.

Butter a 1 ½ quart soufflé dish or casserole.

In a saucepan, scald milk on high heat, add grits, reduce heat to medium-low and cook until thick, stirring constantly, about 10 to 15 minutes. Remove from heat.

Add salt, baking powder, butter, sugar and cheese. Mix well.

Beat egg yolks and add to the grits mixture.

Whip egg whites until they hold soft peaks and fold into the grits mixture.

Pour the mixture into the prepared dish and bake for 30 minutes.

NOTE: The soufflé will rise nicely and if not served immediately, will collapse but will still taste wonderful.

"I'm always looking for side dishes to serve with entrées. Potatoes are good but this southern ingredient cooked with a French method is perfect with pork and beef."

GUACAMOLE IN CRISPY CUPS

MAKES 2 CUPS GUACAMOLE | PREP TIME: 10 MINUTES

- 4 RIPE AVOCADOS
- 1 TBSP FRESH LEMON JUICE
- 1 JALAPEÑO PEPPER, DICED VERY SMALL
- ½ CUP RED ONION, DICED
- ½ CUP CILANTRO, CHOPPED
- 1 CUP POMEGRANATE SEEDS
- 1 TSP SALT
- 1 TSP PEPPER
- WONTON CUPS FOR SERVING

Cut the avocados in half, remove the pits and scoop the flesh out into a bowl.

Add the lemon juice and toss well.

Using a fork or potato masher, mash the avocados until they are the texture you prefer.

Add the red onion, jalapeño pepper and cilantro and mix well. Fold in the pomegranate seeds.

Add salt and pepper to taste.

To serve, spoon guacamole into wonton cups, recipe on page 251.

NOTE: To prevent guacamole from getting dark before serving, put a piece of plastic wrap on top, touching the guacamole all over so that no air touches the surface.

WINE PAIRING: Monte De Oro Winery | Nostimo | Slightly sweet with tastes of peaches, pineapple and lemon accented by honeysuckle and grapefruit blossoms.

“THESE LITTLE WONTON CUPS ARE EASY TO MAKE AND LOOK SO FESTIVE THAT I USE THEM OFTEN.”

WONTON CUPS

MAKES 24 WONTON CUPS | PREP TIME: 5 MINUTES | COOK TIME: 10 MINUTES

24 WONTON WRAPPERS

COOKING SPRAY

¼ TSP SALT

Preheat the oven to 375°F.

Spray two mini muffin tins with cooking spray.

Spray the wonton wrappers with the oil and place each wrapper into a section of a mini muffin tin. Press into the tin to form a cup. Sprinkle lightly with salt and bake for 8 to 10 minutes, until browned and crisp.

Remove from the tin and cool on a baking rack.

"During the holidays, I fill the wonton cups with the guacamole that includes bright red pomegranate seeds, recipe on page 248 ."

OAK MOUNTAIN WINERY

HOME TO THE FIRST AND ONLY SUBTERRANEAN MINED WINE CAVE IN SOUTHERN CALIFORNIA.

In 2000, Steve and Valerie Andrews purchased their Temecula Hills Estate overlooking Diamond Valley with the desire to make the best wines possible. In 2005, they opened Oak Mountain Winery on the De Portola Wine Trail in Temecula. As the winery expanded, Steve and Valerie Andrews dug the first and only subterranean mined wine cave in Southern California, allowing them to better utilize their land, creating the ideal conditions for barrel-aging wine.

The Andrews family consider all their wine unique and decadent. Their wines are created from classic warm-weather Mediterranean varieties including Mourvedre, Viognier, Grenache, Cabernet Sauvignon, Syrah, Zinfandel and Sangiovese Brunello. Their Temecula Hills Collection features some of their original wines like their bold and refined Reserve Cabernet Sauvignon while their Windy Ridge Cellar Collection wines are sweet and fruit forward. Their Oak Mountain label wines include Steve's popular Tempranillo and Muscat Canelli. They are known for their raspberry and strawberry sparkling wines and also sell avocado oils and balsamic vinegars.

Steve and Valerie Andrews make great wines and graciously host visitors at their lovely winery. Oak Mountain Winery produces 5,500 cases of wine a year. They also have a distillery in the original tasting room on the property where drinks are served in a Prohibition Era setting.

OAK MOUNTAIN
WINERY
PINOTAGE
2015
TEMECULA VALLEY

JAMBALAYA

SERVES 8 | PREP TIME: 20 MINUTES | COOK TIME: 35 MINUTES

¼ CUP BUTTER

3 TBSP OLIVE OIL

1 ½ LB SHRIMP, PEELED AND DEVEINED

1 ½ LB BONELESS, SKINLESS CHICKEN, CUT INTO 1 ½ INCH CUBES

1 ONION, COARSELY CHOPPED

1 GREEN BELL PEPPER, COARSELY CHOPPED

3 RIBS CELERY, COARSELY CHOPPED

3 CLOVES GARLIC, FINELY CHOPPED

1 JALAPEÑO, FINELY CHOPPED

4 TOMATOES, PEELED, SEEDED AND CHOPPED

½ TSP DRIED THYME

¼ TSP PAPRIKA

2 CUPS LONG GRAIN WHITE RICE

4 CUPS CHICKEN BROTH

Preheat oven to 350°F.

Heat the butter with 1 tbsp of the olive oil. Add the shrimp and cook until opaque, about 3 minutes per side. Transfer to a platter and reserve.

Add the chicken to the pan and sauté until browned, about 5 minutes. Transfer to the platter with the shrimp and reserve.

Add the remaining 2 tbsp of olive oil. Add the onion, bell pepper and celery (the Creole Holy Trinity) and sauté until softened but not browned. Add the garlic and jalapeño and cook for a minute.

Stir in the chopped tomatoes, thyme, paprika, rice, broth, bay leaves, Worcestershire sauce, ham and sausage. Mix well. Bring the jambalaya to a boil, cover and put in the oven, until the rice is tender, about 20 to 25 minutes.

Add the shrimp, chicken and green onions and let stand for 5 minutes to warm through.

WINE PAIRING: Oak Mountain Winery | Pinotage | A succulent wine with rich aromas of banana, mocha coffee and toffee. Plum and nutty flavors are delivered on the palate.

3 BAY LEAVES

2 TBSP WORCESTERSHIRE SAUCE

½ LB ANDOUILLE SAUSAGE OR KIELBASA, SLICED ¼ INCH THICK

½ LB SMOKED HAM, CUT INTO ½ INCH CUBES

1 BUNCH GREEN ONIONS, SLICED, WHITE AND PART OF GREEN

SALT TO TASTE

Serve in bowls with crusty French bread.

"I came to appreciate the dishes of Louisiana when I lived there (nothing beats crawfish on the levee though). This rice dish originated two hundred years ago in the port city of New Orleans and this version always includes tomatoes. The second version from other parts of Louisiana is brown with no tomatoes."

NEW ORLEANS BREAD PUDDING

SERVES 6 TO 8 | PREP TIME: 20 MINUTES | COOK TIME: 50 MINUTES

PUDDING

1 CUP SUGAR

8 TBSP BUTTER, ROOM TEMPERATURE

5 EGGS, BEATEN

2 CUPS HEAVY CREAM

DASH CINNAMON

1 TBSP VANILLA EXTRACT

¼ CUP RAISINS

FRENCH BAGUETTE, CUT INTO 1 INCH CUBES

Continued on page 260

Preheat oven to 350°F.

Butter a 9 inch square pan.

Cream together the sugar and butter. Add eggs, cream, cinnamon, vanilla and raisins and mix well. Pour into prepared pan

Arrange bread flat in the custard mixture and let stand for 5 minutes to soak up some of the liquid. Turn bread over and let stand for 10 minutes longer. Push the bread down so that it is covered by the custard mixture.

Set the bread pudding pan into a larger baking pan. Fill the baking pan with 1 inch of water and cover with aluminum foil. Bake for 45 to 50 minutes, uncovering the bread pudding for the last 10 minutes to brown the top. When done the custard should be soft.

Serve with Windy Ridge sauce.

Continued on page 260.

WINE PAIRING: Oak Mountain Winery | Bentley's Bubbles | This sparkler is a pale pink Grenache Rosé with aromas of berries and flowers.

WINDY RIDGE SAUCE

1 CUP SUGAR

1 CUP HEAVY CREAM

DASH CINNAMON

1 TBSP BUTTER

½ TSP CORNSTARCH

¼ WATER

¼ CUP WINDY RIDGE DOUBLE TROUBLE RIESLING

In a saucepan, combine sugar, heavy cream, cinnamon and butter. Bring to a boil.

In a small bowl, mix the cornstarch and water. Stir it into the saucepan, cooking until the sauce is translucent. Remove from heat and stir in wine.

"THIS BREAD PUDDING
WITH A RICH CUSTARDY
BOTTOM AND TOASTY
BREAD ON TOP IS TOPPED
WITH A FULL BODIED WINE
SAUCE SETTING IT APART."

PALUMBO FAMILY VINEYARDS AND WINERY

A SIMPLE CONCEPT, COMPLEX WINES.

— Nicholas Palumbo, owner and winemaker, Palumbo Family Vineyards and Winery

Nicholas Palumbo, the winemaker for Palumbo Family Vineyards and Winery maximizes what the land and climate of the Temecula Valley offer. He describes himself as part farmer and part culinary artist. Combining his ancestral leanings toward agriculture from his Sicilian parentage and Illinois farmers, he leans on his artistic talent to turn his estate grown grapes into delectable wines.

In 1998 Nicholas bought seven acres planted with grapes and learned how to grow and harvest with guidance in winemaking from experts. Today, Nicholas produces complex wines with depth of character, specializing in full-bodied reds. Nicholas lives with his wife Cindy and four children on a thirteen-acre estate where their lives center around grapes and winemaking.

They are committed to small lot, handcrafted wines from varieties that are grown on the property. The 13-acre, 2,500 case per year family-run winery has often been described as "boutique" but Nicholas favors the word "artisanal" to describe the involvement and passion that goes into the daily operations.

Nicholas Palumbo is a passionate viticulturist and budding enologist who believes in producing only what he grows himself. "I believe there are only two basic ingredients in making fine wines, the fruit itself and the barrels it ages in." With one foot in modern techniques and the other foot firmly planted in tradition, the wines produced possess a depth and elegance.

Nick and Cindy Palumbo believe the vineyards come first. Their vineyards are planted with Cabernet Sauvignon, Cabernet Franc, Merlot, Sangiovese, Viognier and Syrah varietals. Specializing in full-bodied reds, they offer a few special blends, like their popular Meritage called "Tre Fratelli" and the 2005 Shiraz Cabernet Sauvignon.

The Palumbos' vineyard and winery are certified as sustainable in their ecological practices by utilizing owls and hawks as pest control and purchasing their corks from forests that continue to grow. They also produce olive oil. Cindy has penned several children's books called the Farmer Boy series, teaching children to love the land and what it can produce.

ESTATE
Palumbo Family
VINEYARDS & WINERY
VINTAGE 2014
TRE FRATELLI
Meritage
TEMECULA VALLEY

BUCKWHEAT BLINIS WITH SMOKED SALMON

MAKES 18 PANCAKES | PREP TIME: 10 MINUTES | COOK TIME: 10 MINUTES

⅔ CUP ALL PURPOSE FLOUR

⅓ CUP BUCKWHEAT FLOUR

½ TSP BAKING POWDER

¾ TSP SALT

¾ CUP + 2 TBSP WHOLE MILK

1 LARGE EGG

¼ LB BUTTER, MELTED

½ LB SMOKED SALMON, THINLY SLICED

½ CUP CRÈME FRAÎCHE OR SOUR CREAM

2 TSP FRESH DILL, FINELY CHOPPED

Combine the two flours, baking powder and salt. In a separate bowl, whisk together the milk, egg and 1 tbsp of melted butter, then whisk into the flour mixture.

Heat 1 tbsp of the butter in a sauté pan and drop the batter by tablespoons into the hot skillet. Cook over medium heat until bubbles form on the top side of the blini. Flip and cook for one more minute, until brown. Repeat with the remaining batter, adding additional butter to the pan as needed. Set the blinis aside.

Mix the crème fraîche with the chopped dill.

To serve, top each blini with a dollop of dill crème fraîche and place a piece of salmon on top. Garnish with a sprig of fresh dill.

WINE PAIRING: Palumbo Family Vineyards and Winery | Grenache | Rosewater, cherry juice and cherry blossom aromas are lifted by herbal touches of marjoram and crushed peppercorn. Fennel, thyme and oregano flavors kick off the palate, where strong acidity carries raspberry and red berry flavors into a complex and elegant finish.

CHICKEN PESTO PASTA

SERVES 6 | PREP TIME: 5 MINUTES | COOK TIME: 20 MINUTES

- 1 LB LINGUINI
- 2 TBSP OLIVE OIL
- 2 TBSP BUTTER
- 4 BONELESS, SKINLESS CHICKEN BREASTS
- 2 GARLIC CLOVES, MINCED
- SALT AND PEPPER
- ¾ CUP HEAVY CREAM
- ½ CUP CHICKEN BROTH
- ¼ CUP PESTO
- 3 TBSP PARMESAN, GRATED
- ¼ CUP SUN DRIED TOMATOES, CUT INTO THIN STRIPS
- 12 OZ FRESH BABY SPINACH

Cook pasta al dente according to package directions. Drain, rinse under cold water and reserve.

Sprinkle chicken breasts with salt and pepper. In a large skillet, heat the oil and butter and sauté the chicken breasts with the garlic until the chicken breasts are cooked. Remove chicken to a cutting board and cut into thin strips.

Reduce heat and stir in all remaining ingredients except spinach. Cook until sauce begins to thicken.

Return chicken and pasta to pan and heat through.

Place uncooked spinach in the bottom of a large bowl, and pour pasta mixture over spinach. Toss and serve.

"This is a 'hurry-up and eat' kind of dish with a lot of flavor. The fresh spinach served under the pasta lends freshness."

WINE PAIRING: Palumbo Family Vineyards and Winery | Grenache Blanc | Aromas of light peach, Meyer-lemon peel and yellow flower. Flavors of yellow pear, lemon rinds and stone fruit. Acidity in the finish.

PELTZER FAMILY CELLARS

"A DAY WITH OUT WINE IS LIKE...JUST KIDDING, I HAVE NO IDEA."
— Peltzer Family Cellars

The 25-acre Peltzer Farm and Winery offers great wine and wonderful experiences to people of all ages in a down home farm setting with an industrial-chic mix. The family has been in Southern California since 1924 growing and selling Christmas trees and pumpkins. The Peltzers came to Temecula Valley in 2004 to raise their family in the country. Charlie Pelzer planted three well-suited grape varietals in 2010. These include Italy's famous Sangiovese and Barbera, as well as, the notoriously thicker-skinned French grape, Petite Sirah, to produce small lot, boutique-style wines. Peltzer Family Cellars opened in 2016 in their authentic farm setting where visitors stroll among antique farming equipment scattered artfully throughout the property.

The Peltzers stage huge harvest time family events that include a pumpkin patch, petting zoo, pony rides, and mini-train rides. They open an ice rink during November and December and in Spring they offer Easter Egg Hunts, making their winery a family-fun destination.

They produce 3,500 cases of wine a year.

PELTZER
FAMILY CELLARS
2017
SAUVIGNON
BLANC

SHORT RIB HAND PIES

SERVES 8 | PREP TIME: 15 MINUTES | COOK TIME: 3 HOURS 15 MINUTES

1 ½ LB BONELESS BEEF SHORT RIBS, CUT INTO 1 INCH DICE AND PATTED DRY

SALT AND PEPPER TO SEASON RIBS

2 TBSP OLIVE OIL

¼ LB PROSCIUTTO, CUT INTO ¼ INCH DICE

½ LB SHITAKI MUSHROOMS, CLEANED WITH A DAMP PAPER TOWEL AND CUT INTO HALVES

8 TBSP BUTTER, CUT INTO CUBES

½ CUP PELTZER FAMILY CELLARS, ESTATE BARBERA

1 ½ CUPS BEEF STOCK

1 TSP FRESH THYME LEAVES

1 BAY LEAF

¼ CUP FRESH PARSLEY CHOPPED

1 PACKAGE PUFF PASTRY

1 LARGE EGG, BEATEN WITH 1 TSP WATER

Preheat oven to 325°F.

Heat the olive oil in a heavy pot. Season the beef with salt and pepper.

Brown the beef in batches. Do not crowd the pan. Transfer to a large bowl.

Add the prosciutto to the pan that the beef was browned in. Cook until crisp. Add to the bowl with the beef.

Pour off the excess oil in the pan.

Add the beef and prosciutto back into the pan and add the thyme, bay leaf and mushrooms.

Add the stock and wine to the pan. Bring to a boil and cover the pot.

Place the pot into the oven. Cook until the beef is tender, about 2 to 2 ½ hours. Remove from oven and stir in the parsley.

Increase the oven temperature to 400°F.

Place 2 sheets of puff pastry on a floured surface and cut each sheet into four pieces. Place 3 tbsp of the short rib mixture on one side of each rectangle. Brush the egg mixture around the edges of one side, fold over and press to close. Using a fork, press the tines into the edges of the pie.

Place the pies on a baking sheet lined with parchment paper and bake 30 to 40 minutes.

WINE PAIRING: Peltzer Family Cellars | Estate Barbera | Fruit forward wine with notes of sweet wild cherry, strawberry and vanilla.

CORNISH GAME HENS WITH PROSCIUTTO AND SAGE

SERVES 8 | PREP TIME: 10 MINUTES | COOK TIME: 35 MINUTES

4 CORNISH GAME HENS

8 THIN SLICES PROSCIUTTO

16 FRESH SAGE LEAVES

3 TBSP OLIVE OIL

SALT AND PEPPER

FRESH ROSEMARY SPRIGS

Cut down each side of the backbone of the hen and remove it. This will allow the hen to lie flat. Slide your fingers under the skin of the breast meat and insert a piece of prosciutto and a sage leaf. Repeat on the other side. Slide your fingers under the skin on the leg and thigh and insert prosciutto and fresh sage.

Put the hens on a baking sheet and place a rosemary sprig underneath each one. Brush the hens with the olive oil and season with salt and pepper.

Roast until crispy, about 30 to 40 minutes or until a thermometer inserted into the thigh reads 160°F. Remove from oven and let rest for 10 minutes.

Cut each hen in half lengthwise to make 8 servings.

"Once an exotic menu item, Cornish game hens are now a household ingredient. I love these little birds grilled or roasted. These are especially good enhanced with fresh sage, rosemary and prosciutto."

WINE PAIRING: Peltzer Family Cellars | Pinot Grigio | Flavors of orange blossom, ripe pineapple, banana and hibiscus.

SHRIMP FRITTERS WITH AIOLI

SERVES 8 | PREP TIME: 10 MINUTES | COOK TIME: 15 MINUTES

- 2 EGGS, SEPARATED
- ½ LB SMALL SHRIMP (26/30 COUNT), SHELLED AND DEVEINED
- 1 CUP SCALLIONS, FINELY SLICED
- 1 CUP ZUCCHINI, FINELY DICED
- 1 CLOVE GARLIC, MINCED
- ½ JALAPEÑO PEPPER, MINCED
- 1 CUP ALL PURPOSE FLOUR
- 1 TSP BAKING POWDER
- ½ TSP SMOKED PAPRIKA
- ⅔ CUP BUTTERMILK
- ½ TSP SALT
- ½ TSP PEPPER
- VEGETABLE OIL FOR FRYING

In a large bowl, mix together the flour, baking powder, paprika, salt and pepper.

Whisk in the egg yolks and enough of the buttermilk so the batter is thick and not runny.

Add the shrimp, scallions, zucchini, garlic and jalapeños into the batter. Mix lightly to combine.

In a seperate bowl, whip the egg whites into peaks and fold into the shrimp batter.

Heat about 1 ½ inches of the oil in a heavy bottomed pot until a deep-fry thermometer registers 350°F. Using a small scoop or a spoon, drop a tablespoon of batter into the hot oil. Cook until lightly browned, about 4 to 5 minutes. Drain on paper towels.

Serve with aioli.

"This recipe comes from the time when I lived in Morgan City, Louisiana. Morgan City is deep in the bayou country and they are all about shrimp and petroleum. The city's welcoming statue features a shrimp boat and there is an annual shrimp festival. This is my favorite recipe from that time. The aioli sauce makes a good accompaniment, but you could use a remoulade sauce or a spicy cocktail sauce."

WINE PAIRING: Peltzer Family Cellars | Albariño | Flavors of white nectarine, orange zest, with a touch of sea salt.

AIOLI

8 CLOVES GARLIC, SKIN REMOVED AND FINELY CHOPPED

½ TSP SALT

2 EGG YOLKS

1 TSP RED WINE VINEGAR

1 TBSP FRESH LEMON JUICE

1 CUP OLIVE OIL

Place the chopped garlic in a bowl with the egg yolks, vinegar and lemon juice. Whisk to blend thoroughly.

Gradually add oil, a drop at a time, whisking constantly. You may add oil a little faster when the aioli begins to thicken. Adjust seasoning and refrigerate until ready to use.

PLATEAU VINEYARDS

"WITH WINE, LIFE IS BEAUTIFUL." — George Schaeffer, owner, Plateau Vineyards

Plateau Vineyards is located above the Temecula Valley on the Santa Rosa Plateau. The first grape vines were planted in 1993 in a location blessed with warm and sunny days, afternoon sea breezes, and cool nights, which add up to produce some of the finest wine grapes in California.

Plateau grape varietals include Cabernet Sauvignon, Merlot, Zinfandel, Sauvignon Blanc, Pinot Gris, and Albariño. The grapes are harvested by hand at peak ripeness and are crafted in small batches into our premium estate bottled reds, whites and blends that are sold only in the boutique winery or by online order. They produce 2,500 cases of wine each year.

Plateau Vineyards offers cooking classes and gives garden tours in the nearby Santa Rosa Plateau Nature Preserve.

Plateau
VINEYARDS
2012
CABERNET SAUVIGNON
ESTATE BOTTLED
CALIFORNIA • SOUTH COAST

BEEF SATAY WITH PEANUT SAUCE

SERVES 8 AS A FIRST COURSE | PREP TIME: 30 MINUTES | COOK TIME: 8-10 MINUTES

2 LB SKIRT STEAK, CUT INTO 2 INCH WIDE STRIPS

6 TBSP DARK SOY SAUCE

2 TBSP MOLASSES

2 TBSP BROWN SUGAR

4 GARLIC CLOVES, MINCED

4 TBSP WATER

2 TBSP LIME JUICE

1 CUCUMBER, PEELED AND CUT INTO 1 INCH PIECES

1 LARGE WHITE ONION, CUT INTO 1 INCH WEDGES

24 BAMBOO SKEWERS SOAKED IN WATER FOR 30 MINUTES

Make the marinade by combining soy sauce, molasses, brown sugar, garlic, water and lime juice. Marinade the steak about 30 minutes before grilling.

Thread the marinated beef pieces on the skewers. Grill the satay over a charcoal fire, under a broiler or use a stove top broiling pan.

Serve with peanut sauce, cucumbers and wedges of raw onion.

WINE PAIRING: Plateau Vineyards | Cabernet Sauvignon | This wine displays dark cherry flavors with a hint of cocoa, caramel and vanilla. The beautiful garnet color enhances this well balanced, medium bodied wine.

PEANUT SAUCE

1 TSP SALT

2 GARLIC CLOVES

1 TBSP FRESH GINGER, MINCED

1 STALK LEMONGRASS, OUTER LAYERS REMOVED AND MINCED

2 SHALLOTS, MINCED

3 TBSP VEGETABLE OIL

2 TBSP SUGAR

¼ CUP CREAMY PEANUT BUTTER

½ CUP COCONUT MILK

¼ CUP TAMARIND, ORANGE OR TANGERINE JUICE

Put the salt, garlic cloves, ginger, lemon grass, shallots and vegetable oil into a blender. Blend until smooth.

Put the mixture into a small saucepan and add the sugar, peanut butter, coconut milk and tamarind juice. Stir to mix and heat until the mixture boils and thickens, about 2 minutes.

Store in a glass jar. This will keep for about 2 weeks in the refrigerator.

MAILLE
Depuis 1747 • Since 1747
1747

COUNTRY PÂTÉ

MAKES APPROXIMATELY 2 ½ LB | PREP TIME: 20 MINUTES | COOK TIME: 1 HOUR 30 MINUTES

- 1 LB GROUND BEEF
- 8 OZ PORK SHOULDER, GROUND
- 8 OZ LEAN SMOKED HAM, CUT INTO ¼ INCH DICE
- 1 MEDIUM ONION, DICED
- 2 TBSP OLIVE OIL
- 3 TBSP BRANDY
- 6 SLICES BACON, BLANCHED IN BOILING WATER FOR 2 MINUTES
- ½ TSP THYME
- 1 TSP SALT
- 1 ½ TSP PEPPER
- 2 LARGE EGGS
- 2 BAY LEAVES
- BUTTERED CROUTONS TO SERVE
- CORNICHONS FOR GARNISH

Preheat the oven to 350°F.

Sauté the onions in olive oil. Remove from heat and let cool.

Gently mix the sautéd onions, ground beef, ground pork, seasonings, brandy and eggs in a large mixing bowl. Fold in the diced ham.

Place the blanched bacon in a 6 cup loaf pan, making 3 rows of bacon, evenly spaced across the pan, 2 slices of bacon in each row. This will leave enough bacon to overlap on the top.

Spoon the meat mixture into the prepared pan. Place the bay leaves on top and fold over the bacon. Cover the loaf pan with a piece of foil and cut several slits in it to allow for escaping steam.

Place the loaf pan in a larger baking pan filled with 1 inch of hot water and put into the oven for 1 ½ hours or until a meat thermometer reads 160°F. The juices of the pâté will run clear when it is cooked.

Remove from water bath and cool. The pâté can be made 2 or 3 days ahead, wrapped tightly in plastic wrap and refrigerated.

To serve, place a slice of the pâté on a buttered crouton and top with half a cornichon that has been cut into a fan shape.

"When they hear 'pâté' most people think of liver. This country pâté has no liver and is really a French meatloaf. Serve as an appetizer or on a baguette with mustard and aioli for a delicious sandwich."

WINE PAIRING: Plateau Vineyards | Merlot | Exhibits velvety raspberry, blackberry and cherry undertones with a trace of currant and a hint of tobacco.

POGGIO LEANO

PROUD TO SHARE OLD WORLD ITALIAN INFLUENCE AND FLAVOR.

—Alex Prestifilippo, owner and winemaker, Poggio Leano

The Poggio Leano Wine Room and Lounge is just a small part of the Prestifilippo Family enterprises. Understanding that for over 2,000 years, Italy has produced some of the most favorite wines in the world, Alex Prestifilippo stays true to his Sicilian roots using authentic Old World farming methods. He says he adds passion from his heart and hands to harvest his grapes and olives and to produce fine wines and olive oils and is proud to share some Old World Italian influence and flavor.

The Prestifilippo family began planting in 2003. Their vineyards include, Leccino, Biancolilla Di Sicilia, Nocellara Del Belice, Frantoio, Pendolino, Sevillano, Sangiovese, Cabernet Sauvignon, Syrah, Nero d'Avola, Malbec, Pinot Noir, Catarratto and Muscato Canelli grapes, Arbequina Olives, along with a vast variety of fruits and vegetables.

Alex carefully matches root stock and clones to the soil for optimal results and produces 3,000 cases of wine per year.

Poggio Leano
2017
Temecula Valley
Cabernet Sauvignon
ALCOHOL 15.5% BY VOLUME

SAN FRANCISCO CIOPPINO

SERVES 6 | PREP TIME: 25 MINUTES | COOK TIME: 40 MINUTES

3 TBSP OLIVE OIL

1 ½ CUPS ONION, SLICED

2 TBSP GARLIC, MINCED

¼ CUP TOMATO PASTE

1 CUP WHITE WINE

1 ¼ CUPS CRUSHED CANNED TOMATOES

2 TBSP ITALIAN PARSLEY LEAVES

1 TBSP FRESH THYME LEAVES, MINCED

1 BAY LEAF

¼ CUP BASIL LEAVES, JULIENNED

Continued on next page

Heat the oil in a heavy pan. Add the onion, cook for 10 minutes, then add garlic and cook until onions are translucent.

Add stock, tomatoes, tomato paste, wine, parsley, thyme, basil and bay leaf. Simmer for 10 minutes.

Add mussels, clams, shrimp, scallops and fish. Cover until shellfish open and fish is cooked through, about 5 to 10 minutes.

Taste for seasoning and serve.

WINE PAIRING: Poggio Leano | Cabernet Sauvignon | The Italian styling produces a dark red wine with aromas of fruit, cinnamon and oak with flavors of blackberry, red currant, hazelnut and pepper.

3 CUPS FISH STOCK OR 1 CUP CLAM JUICE MIXED WITH 2 CUPS CHICKEN BROTH

12 MUSSELS

12 CLAMS

1 LB SHRIMP, PEELED AND DEVEINED

12 OZ SCALLOPS

1 LB FIRM FLESHED FISH (SUCH AS, HALIBUT OR SEA BASS), CUT INTO 6 FILETS

OPTIONAL: 2 DUNGENESS OR SNOW CRAB LEGS

SALT AND PEPPER

"By all accounts this fish stew originated in San Francisco and is closely related to regional Italian fish stews. Be sure to serve crusty bread to sop up the sauce."

CASSEROLE OF LENTILS AND SPARERIBS

SERVES 6 TO 8 | PREP TIME: 10 MINUTES | COOK TIME: 1 HOUR

- 2 CUPS LENTILS, WASHED
- 6 CUPS WATER
- 2 ½ TO 3 LB COUNTRY SPARERIBS
- 2 TBSP OLIVE OIL
- 1 ½ CUPS MIREPOIX (⅓ CUP EACH OF CARROT, ONION, AND CELERY, FINELY DICED)
- 3 TBSP FLOUR
- ½ CUP WHITE WINE
- 1 ½ CUPS BEEF STOCK
- 1 BAY LEAF
- ¼ TSP FRESH THYME
- SALT AND PEPPER
- 3 TBSP SHALLOTS, MINCED
- 3 TBSP PARSLEY, MINCED
- ¼ CUP BREAD CRUMBS

Place the lentils in a large saucepan, add the water and bring to a simmer. Maintain the slow heat 10 to 15 minutes, until barely tender. Drain and set aside.

Preheat oven to 375°F.

Dry the spareribs with paper towels and season with salt and pepper. Put the olive oil in a large sauté pan and brown the ribs on all sides. Remove to a platter. Reserve 2 tbsp of oil from the pan to finish the dish.

Add the mirepoix to the pan and sauté until limp. Add the flour and stir constantly for 2 minutes. Whisk in the wine, then the stock and simmer for 5 minutes. Add the bay leaf, thyme, salt and pepper. Remove from heat.

Butter a 9 × 12 inch baking pan. Fold the lentils and the sauce together and pour into the baking dish. Arrange the browned spareribs on top of the lentils. Sprinkle the bread crumbs over the top of the casserole. Drizzle reserved 2 tbsp of oil over the bread crumbs.

Place in the oven for about 40 minutes. The sauce should be thick and bubbling and the bread crumbs nicely browned.

"This is comfort food prepared with a classic method. Cooking the spareribs this way is not the usual but produces a wonderful flavor for the dish."

WINE PAIRING: Poggio Leano | Syrah | Dark ruby in color with complex aromas of black currant and black cherries integrated with silky tannins and flavors of jammy blackberries, white pepper, nutmeg and toasty oak.

CRANBERRY BISCOTTI WITH PISTACHIOS

MAKES 24 | PREP TIME: 10 MINUTES | COOK TIME: 1 HOUR 10 MINUTES

- 1 TSP BAKING POWDER
- 2 ½ CUPS ALL PURPOSE FLOUR
- 1 ¼ CUPS SUGAR
- ⅛ TSP SALT
- 3 LARGE EGGS
- 2 LARGE EGG YOLKS
- 1 TSP. VANILLA EXTRACT
- 1 CUP DRIED CRANBERRIES
- 1 CUP RAW PISTACHIOS, SHELLED
- ZEST OF ONE LEMON

Preheat oven to 350°F.

In an electric mixer fitted with the paddle attachment, combine baking powder, flour, sugar and salt. In a separate bowl, beat eggs, yolks and vanilla and add to the dry ingredients. Mix on medium-low until sticky dough is formed. Stir in nuts, cranberries and zest

Turn out dough onto a well-floured surface. Sprinkle the dough with flour and slightly knead. Divide the dough into 3 equal portions and shape firmly into 9 × 2 ½ inch logs. Transfer to baking sheet lined with parchment paper. Bake until golden brown, 25 to 30 minutes. Remove from oven and turn oven down to 275°F.

Cool logs and cut into ½ inch slices. Return pieces cut side down to baking sheet. Bake until lightly toasted, about 15 to 20 minutes. Turn over. Bake again about 15 to 20 minutes until lightly toasted. Cool on wire rack. Store in an airtight container.

Serve with Poggio Leano Syrah or Poggio Leano Moscato.

WINE PAIRING: Poggio Leano | Moscato | A sweet dry wine made from Muscat Canelli grapes. It boasts flavors of citrus.

PONTE WINERY

IF YOU LIKE IT, IT'S GOOD WINE. – The Ponte Family

Ponte Winery sits in the middle of 300 acres of some of the first vineyards in the Temecula Valley, planted by Brookside Winery in the 1960s. Claudio Ponte has farmed 23 varieties since 1984 on the largest vineyard in Temecula, including Cabernet, Zinfandel, Sangiovese, Pinot Grigio, Vermentino, and Arneis. The vineyard team keeps up to date on viticulture techniques and works hard to make sure the grapes thrive.

The Ponte Winery opened in 2003. In 2011 they became the first winery in the Temecula Valley to achieve the Certified California Sustainable Winegrower designation, continuing in sustainable principles in farming and water usage. They produce 22,000 cases of wine a year as a boutique producer, making wines in very small batches, typically 1,500 cases per year for each variety, which allows them to concentrate on superior quality.

P·O·N·T·E
Winery
Pas Doux
2018

SHRIMP BISQUE

SERVES 8 | PREP TIME: 10 MINUTES | COOK TIME: 40 MINUTES

1 LB SHRIMP

2 TBSP OLIVE OIL

¼ CUP + 1 TBSP BRANDY

¾ CUP ONION, CHOPPED

¾ CUP CARROT, CHOPPED

1 LEEK, COARSELY CHOPPED (WHITE PART ONLY)

2 LARGE TOMATOES, CHOPPED

2 TBSP TOMATO PASTE

1 TSP FRESH THYME (OR ½ TSP DRIED)

1 TBSP FRESH TARRAGON, CHOPPED (OR 1 TSP DRIED)

1 ¾ CUP WHITE WINE

2 TSP SALT

1 TSP BLACK PEPPER

2 CUPS CHICKEN STOCK

2 CUPS CREAM

1 CUP MILK

1 TBSP BUTTER

Shell and devein the shrimp. Chop the shells and reserve.

Chop the shrimp and reserve 4 tbsp of the shrimp.

In a large sauté pan add the olive oil and when hot, add the chopped shrimp shells. Cook for 5 minutes, stirring often. Add the ¼ cup brandy and ignite. When the flames die down, add the onion, carrot, leek, tomatoes, tomato paste, thyme, tarragon, white wine, salt, pepper and chicken stock. Bring to a boil, reduce heat and simmer for about 20 minutes.

Strain the soup through a metal sieve, pushing with a spoon to extract as much liquid as possible.

Put the soup back into the pot and add the cream and milk. Bring to a boil, add the chopped shrimp and simmer until the shrimp are cooked through, about 3 to 4 minutes.

Taste for seasoning and stir in the 1 tbsp brandy.

In a small sauté pan, melt the butter. Add the 4 tbsp of reserved shrimp and sauté until cooked through.

Serve hot with the chopped shrimp meat over the top.

"A creamy and rich dish that is an alternative to lobster bisque and the fresh tarragon, wine and brandy elevate this soup to party status. Serve in bowls or in mini cups for an appetizer."

WINE PAIRING: Ponte Winery | Pastorello | A medium bodied wine with lush aromas of white peach and jasmine. Flavors of passion fruit and a hint of sea salt.

PONTE WINERY

MEXICAN CHOCOLATE PIE

SERVES 8 | PREP TIME: 15 MINUTES | COOK TIME: 10 MINUTES

CRUST

5 WHOLE GRAHAM CRACKERS

¾ CUP SLICED ALMONDS, PUREED TO A MEALY TEXTURE OR ½ CUP ALMOND MEAL

2 OZ BUTTER, MELTED

FILLING

1 CUP HEAVY CREAM

¾ TABLET MEXICAN CHOCOLATE, BROKEN UP

1 ½ CUPS DARK CHOCOLATE, CHOPPED

1 ½ CUPS WHIPPING CREAM, WHIPPED AND CHILLED

To make the crust, put the graham crackers into a food processor and process to a coarse meal. Put into a bowl and add the almond meal and melted butter. Press the crust mixture into a 10 inch pie pan.

To make the filling, in a saucepan, heat the cream until boiling. Lower the heat and add the Mexican chocolate. Stir until it melts and then add the 1 ½ cups of dark chocolate and stir to melt until smooth. Remove from heat. Cool to room temperature.

Fold the 1 ½ cups whipped cream into the cooled chocolate. Spoon the chocolate mixture into the prepared pie shell. Refrigerate for at least 2 hours.

NOTE: 1 ounce semi-sweet chocolate, ½ teaspoon cinnamon and 1 drop of almond extract can be substituted for Mexican chocolate.

If you like, you can whip additional whipped cream and add it as a topping to the pie.

WINE PAIRING: Ponte Winery | Late Harvest | A blend of red grapes picked late in the harvest. A balanced, sweet wine boasting flavors of berries, licorice and toasted marshmallow.

MUSSELS AND FENNEL IN SAFFRON CREAM SAUCE

SERVES 6 | PREP TIME: 20 MINUTES | COOK TIME: 40 MINUTES

4 ½ LB SMALL MUSSELS, RINSED AND SCRUBBED

1 (750 ML) BOTTLE OF PONTE PINOT GRIGIO

½ CUP WATER

3 TBSP EXTRA VIRGIN OLIVE OIL

1 BOUQUET GARNI (COMPOSED OF 1 SPRIG FRESH THYME, 1 BAY LEAF AND SEVERAL SPRIGS OF PARSLEY TIED IN CHEESE CLOTH)

3 SMALL CARROTS, PEELED AND JULIENNED

1 SWEET RED PEPPER, CORED WITH SEEDS REMOVED AND JULIENNED

1 BULB FRESH FENNEL, TRIMMED AND JULIENNED

½ TSP SAFFRON

6 LARGE EGG YOLKS

1 ¼ CUP CRÈME FRAÎCHE

3 TBSP PARSLEY, COARSELY CHOPPED

SALT AND PEPPER

In a large pot, combine the wine, 6 tbsp water, mussels and bouquet garni. Cover and simmer over high heat for about 5 minutes. Check and stir often and remove from heat when all mussels are open.

Place olive oil in a large skillet. Add the carrots, peppers and fennel. Sauté over medium heat until tender. Set aside.

Remove mussels from the pot, keeping the broth. Open the mussels and keep the half of the shell to which the meat is attached and discard the other half.

Arrange the mussels on a deep oven-proof platter, spread the vegetables over the top, cover with aluminum foil and set aside.

In a large mixing bowl, combine the egg yolks, crème fraîche and saffron and whisk until blended.

Strain the mussel broth through a fine sieve lined with cheese cloth. Leave some of the broth in the bottom of the pan as that will contain the sandy residue.

Continued on next page.

WINE PAIRING: Ponte Winery | Chardonnay | Notes of luscious ripe peach mid-palate, citrus entry and a pineapple finish.

Preheat oven to 400°F.

Place the platter of mussels in the oven and reheat for 5 minutes.

Pour the mussel broth into a large skillet and bring to a boil. Remove from the heat and pour the broth in a thin steady stream in the egg-cream mixture whisking constantly. Return the mixture to the skillet and simmer over low heat, whisking constantly until the sauce thickens; do not let it boil. Taste for seasoning.

Pour the sauce over the mussels, sprinkle with parsley and serve.

Robert Renzoni
VINEYARDS
2018
VERMENTINO
TEMECULA VALLEY

ROBERT RENZONI VINEYARDS

EVERYTHING WE DO IS BASED ON FAMILY TRADITIONS AND ON THE LAND WHERE THE GRAPES ARE GROWN.

—Robert Renzoni, owner and winemaker, Robert Renzoni Vineyards

Robert Renzoni Vineyards is a tribute to Robert Renzoni's forebearers. His great-grandfather Federico started working in vineyards near the Adriatic Sea in 1886. In 1933 Federico started a wine distribution business in Buffalo, New York, importing wines from Italy and France for many decades. Robert gained experience working in the family business and after moving to Temecula, in 2006 he bought winery property with mature vines.

Ten of the twelve acres of Robert Renzoni Vineyards are planted in classic Bordeaux and Italian grape varieties in six vineyard blocks that produce low yields with concentrated flavors. Growing Cabernet Sauvignon, Pinot Grigio, Sangiovese, Brunello and Barbera, Robert Renzoni Vineyards uses environmentally friendly practices and plants according to the contours of the land. Most are planted with vertical trellising to allow a canopy for good light penetration and a beneficial ratio of leaves to berries.

Robert Renzoni Vineyards opened in 2008 surrounded by rolling hills and olive trees. Robert says everything they do is based on family traditions and on the land where the grapes are grown.

They produce 15,000 cases of wine a year.

PARSLIED CHICKEN NUGGETS WITH SAUCE GRIBICHE

SERVES 6 | PREP TIME: 15 MINUTES | COOK TIME: 10 MINUTES

½ CUP ALL PURPOSE FLOUR

1 TSP SALT

1 BUNCH FRESH PARSLEY, FINELY CHOPPED

1 CUP PANKO BREAD CRUMBS

1 LARGE EGG

1 TBSP WATER

2 WHOLE BONELESS, SKINLESS CHICKEN BREASTS, CUT INTO 1 ½ INCH STRIPS

1 CUP VEGETABLE OIL

SAUCE GRIBICHE

1 CUP MAYONNAISE

1 TBSP CORNICHONS, FINELY CHOPPED

1 TBSP CAPERS, CHOPPED

1 TBSP SHALLOTS, CHOPPED

3 SPRIGS PARSLEY, MINCED

6 FRESH TARRAGON LEAVES, CHOPPED

⅓ TBSP CHIVES, CHOPPED

Place the flour in a resealable bag and add the chicken pieces. Shake to distribute the flour all over the chicken. Put the chicken on a tray and season with salt and pepper.

Whisk the egg and 1 tbsp water in a bowl big enough to dip the chicken pieces in. Combine the bread crumbs and parsley in a separate bowl.

Heat the vegetable oil in a sauté pan.

Dip the flour-coated chicken pieces into the egg wash and then into the bread crumbs, pressing firmly so that the crumbs adhere.

Cook the chicken pieces in the hot oil, browning on all sides, about 8 minutes total.

Remove the chicken to a paper lined tray to drain. Keep warm.

Serve with sauce gribiche.

To make the sauce gribiche, combine all ingredients thoroughly and refrigerate until ready to use.

WINE PAIRING: Robert Renzoni Vineyards | Pinot Grigio | Flavors of ripened pear, Granny Smith apple and lemon zest with a rich finish.

POLENTA WITH PANCETTA AND ROSEMARY

SERVES 6 TO 8 | PREP TIME: 5 MINUTES | COOK TIME: 40 MINUTES

3 TBSP OLIVE OIL

6 OZ PANCETTA

5 CUPS WATER

½ TSP SALT

2 ⅓ CUPS CORNMEAL

2 TBSP FRESH ROSEMARY, CHOPPED

Preheat oven to 350°F.

In a sauté pan, combine 2 tbsp of olive oil and pancetta. Sauté until pancetta is crisp. Remove and reserve.

In a deep saucepan, bring the water to a boil and add salt. Slowly add the cornmeal in a thin, steady stream, stirring constantly. Cook for about 20 minutes over low heat, stirring constantly until polenta thickens.

Oil an 8 × 12 inch baking dish. Line the bottom with half of the pancetta.

Cover the pancetta with the polenta, smoothing the surface with a wet knife. Arrange the remaining pancetta on top and sprinkle with the chopped rosemary. Drizzle the remaining olive oil over the top.

Bake until the top is golden, about 20 minutes.

"Accompanied by a glass of wine and a green salad, such as, the Romaine Salad with Roasted Poblano Dressing (recipe on page 35), this makes an interesting and satisfying meal. As a hearty side dish, it pairs well with chicken, beef and pork (Pork Chops Braised with Sage and Tomatoes, (recipe on page 32)."

WINE PAIRING: Robert Renzoni Vineyards | Old Vine Zinfandel | Well-structured and balanced, this wine offers brilliant aromas of ripe blackberry, coffee and caramel, accented by soft black pepper.

SCALLOPS WITH ROASTED BRUSSELS SPROUTS

SERVES 4 | PREP TIME: 10 MINUTES | COOK TIME: 20 MINUTES

- 12 FRESH SCALLOPS
- ½ CUP ALL PURPOSE FLOUR
- 3 TBSP BUTTER, UNSALTED
- 3 CLOVES GARLIC, FINELY MINCED
- 2 TBSP FRESH PARSLEY, FINELY CHOPPED
- 1 ½ TSP WORCESTERSHIRE SAUCE
- 3 TBSP LEMON JUICE
- 1 ½ TSP BRANDY
- 12 BRUSSELS SPROUTS, TRIMMED AND HALVED
- 3 OZ PANCETTA CUT INTO ¼ INCH DICE
- SPRAY OLIVE OIL
- 1 LARGE SHALLOT, THINLY SLICED AND LIGHTLY FRIED FOR GARNISH.

Preheat oven to 425°F.

Arrange brussels sprouts, cut side down on a baking sheet.

Sprinkle the pancetta over the sprouts and spray generously with olive oil. Bake for 20 minutes or until tender.

While the brussels sprouts are cooking prepare the scallops. Dry the scallops thoroughly. Salt and pepper the scallops and dust lightly with flour.

In a large skillet, melt the butter and sauté the scallops until they are golden on both sides.

Add the garlic, parsley, Worcestershire sauce and lemon juice.

Mix gently together in the pan. Add the brandy and flame it quickly.

Serve over the brussels sprouts. Top with a few of the crispy shallots.

WINE PAIRING: Robert Renzoni Vineyards | Vermentino | Flavors of apricots, white peach, mandarin orange and various tropical fruits with fresh acidity on the finish.

SOMERSET VINEYARD AND WINERY

SOMERSET IS THE ONLY WINERY OFFERING MACABEO WINES IN THE TEMECULA VALLEY.

The name of Somerset Vineyard and Winery celebrates happy times founders Kurt and John Tiedt spent with good friends growing up on Somerset Street in Orange County. The vineyards of Zinfandel and Grenache grapes at Somerset were planted thirty years ago by Carl Keys for his Keyways Winery. In 2006 Terri Lee Pedley Delhamer purchased the property and planted additional varietals. The sustainably farmed 13-acres now bear Rhone varietals as well as Spanish Macabeo, Monastrell, and Tempranillo, producing outstanding quality grapes and wine. Somerset is the only winery offering Macabeo wines in the Temecula Valley. They presently produce about 6,000 cases of wine each year.

The Tiedts invite others to come to Somerset to share their wines good times. They hope their setting will encourage people to tell their stories, to laugh, sing, and dance, to prolong the joy of friendship, the thrill of life and the taste for fun.

SOMERSET
winery
ESTATE
Tempranillo
2014
TEMECULA VALLEY

PORK TENDERLOIN WITH CRANBERRIES

SERVES 6 | PREP TIME: 10 MINUTES | COOK TIME: 1 HOUR 10 MINUTES

2 (1 LB) PORK TENDERLOINS

1 TBSP OLIVE OIL

SALT AND PEPPER

3 CUPS ONION, SLICED ¼ INCH THICK

1 CUP RED WINE

1 CUP CHICKEN BROTH

½ CUP DRIED CRANBERRIES

Season pork with salt and pepper. Heat oil in a large, deep skillet. Add pork, browning on all sides. Remove pork from pan. Add the onion to the pan, reduce the heat and cook for 8 minutes or until browned. Remove onion from pan and season lightly with salt and pepper. Add wine to pan, cook over high heat until reduced to ½ cup.

Return pork and onion to pan with the wine reduction. Add chicken broth and bring to a boil.

Cover, reduce heat and simmer 30 minutes.

Stir in cranberries, cover and cook for 15 minutes or until pork is tender. Remove from heat. Place pork on a cutting board and let stand 5 minutes. Slice pork and serve with onion cranberry sauce.

"This is a very flavorful rendition of pork tenderloin. Nice any time and pretty for holidays."

Serve with the Roasted Sweet Potatoes with Asparagus, recipe on page 315.

WINE PAIRING: Somerset Vineyard and Winery | Cabernet Franc | Aromas of raspberry, black currant, violets with a slight pepper zest. Flavors of cherries, tomato and dried oregano. This wine can be aged.

ROASTED SWEET POTATOES WITH ASPARAGUS

SERVES 8 | PREP TIME: 10 MINUTES | COOK TIME: 25 MINUTES

2 LARGE SWEET POTATOES, PEELED AND CUT INTO 8 WEDGES EACH

16 STALKS FRESH ASPARAGUS, TRIMMED

2 TBSP SPRAY OLIVE OIL OR VEGETABLE OIL

Preheat oven to 450°F.

Spray potatoes and asparagus with olive oil or vegetable spray.

Place potatoes on a foiled lined baking sheet and put into the oven for 15 minutes.

Add asparagus to baking sheet and roast for another 10 minutes.

Serve with the Pork Tenderloin with Cranberries, recipe on page 312.

SHERRY APPLE CAKE

SERVES 10 TO 12 | PREP TIME: 15 MINUTES | COOK TIME: 1 HOUR 30 MINUTES

1 CUP BUTTER, ROOM TEMPERATURE + 1 TBSP FOR CAKE PAN

2 CUPS SUGAR

3 EGGS, ROOM TEMPERATURE

3 CUPS FLOUR + 2 TBSP FOR CAKE PAN

1 ½ TSP BAKING SODA

½ TSP SALT

1 TSP CINNAMON

⅛ TSP NUTMEG

3 CUPS APPLES, PEELED AND CUT INTO 1 INCH DICE

2 CUPS WALNUTS OR PECANS, CHOPPED

2 TSP VANILLA

SHERRY GLAZE

½ CUP SUGAR

½ CUP SHERRY

Preheat oven to 325°F.

Butter and flour a 10 inch cake pan.

In a bowl, mix together the flour, baking soda, salt, cinnamon and nutmeg.

In a seperate bowl, cream butter and sugar until well blended. Add the eggs one at a time, beating after each addition. Gradually add the dry ingredients to the butter and eggs. Add the apples, nuts and vanilla. Pour into the prepared cake pan. Bake about 1 ½ hours or until a toothpick inserted into the middle comes out clean.

Let stand 15 minutes and turn out.

To make the glaze, mix together ingredients and stir constantly over low heat until syrupy, then pour over warm cake.

"This has been in my repertoire for a long time and was the most requested cake at my first restaurant in Fallbrook California. It is especially tasty at apple season when the fruit is at its best."

WINE PAIRING: Somerset Vineyard and Winery | Late Harvest Roussanne | Intense and sweet with flavors of apricot, mandarin orange, tropical fruit and spiced crème brûlée. It finishes with a lively acidity and crispness.

SOUTH COAST WINERY
WINEMAKER'S SIGNATURE SELECTION
SPARKLING PINOT GRIGIO
TEMECULA VALLEY

SOUTH COAST WINERY RESORT & SPA

SOUTH COAST'S WINES ARE "MADE THE WAY PEOPLE WANT TO DRINK IT".

South Coast Winery Resort & Spa is the result of founder Jim Carter's vision for creating a winery experience after seeing the movie "A Walk in the Clouds". In 1981, Jim Carter purchased 400 acres in Temecula Valley. He planted and nurtured the finest grapes and added expert winemakers to the team to build the South Coast Winery Resort & Spa. He added villas for overnight stays and The Vineyard Rose Lounge restaurant in the middle of 63 acres.

Since first bottling wine in 2003, South Coast Winery has earned more than 3,000 awards in regional and international competitions. Their Cabernet Sauvignon, Cabernet Blanc, Petite Sirah, Zinfandel, and Chardonnay lead the list of their award winners. South Coast Winery is the first winery among 750 to receive the title of California Winery of the Year four times from the California State Fair Wine Competition, the oldest and most prestigious wine competition in the United States dating to 1854.

South Coast produces 8,000 cases of charmat process sparkling wine each year aged in stainless steel tanks and 45,000 cases of table wine. The South Coast vineyards are on the eastern side of Mount Palomar and set in the native terrain of Southern California where the daytime heat and nighttime cold is ideal for winegrowing.

After tasting his first harvest, Carter realized his mountain vineyard had something extra—more sunshine. Carter's vineyards are planted in 3'6" heights, allowing the extra sunshine to meet and make each cluster of grapes full of flavor. Visitors may take "Behind the Scenes Wine Tours" to experience the winemaking process from grape to glass.

GAI

GULF CRAB CAKES WITH REMOULADE

MAKES 12 TO 15 CAKES | PREP TIME: 25 MINUTES | COOK TIME: 10 MINUTES

CRAB CAKES

1 RED BELL PEPPER, FINELY DICED

1 BUNCH GREEN ONIONS, CHOPPED

2 EGGS

¾ CUP MAYONNAISE

1 TBSP WORCESTERSHIRE SAUCE

1 TSP HOT SAUCE

1 TSP CREOLE SEASONING

1 LB CRAB CLAW MEAT

1 LB JUMBO LUMP CRABMEAT

2 CUPS PANKO BREAD CRUMBS

½ TSP SALT

¼ CUP CANOLA, VEGETABLE OR PEANUT OIL FOR FRYING

To make the crab cakes, mix together bell pepper, green onions, eggs, mayonnaise, Worcestershire, hot sauce, creole seasoning and salt.

Gently fold in crab meat, trying not to break up the big pieces. Form into small cakes, about ⅓ cup each, slightly flatten.

Put the bread crumbs into a shallow dish and gently coat the outside of each cake with the crumbs.

In a sauté pan, heat the oil until it shimmers. Carefully fry the crab cakes and drain on paper towels.

Serve hot with remoulade sauce.

"There are a lot of crab cake recipes but my students swear that these are the best they've ever tasted and I agree."

WINE PAIRING: South Coast Winery Resort & Spa | Sauvignon Blanc | This wine is a cornucopia of flavors and aromas: sweet kiwi and lime, gooseberries, pears, passion fruit and wild flowers with a finish of crisp acidity.

REMOULADE

¼ CUP MAYONNAISE

1 TBSP SHALLOTS, CHOPPED

1 ½ TBSP CAPERS, DRAINED AND CHOPPED

2 TSP DIJON MUSTARD

1 TSP FRESH LEMON JUICE

SALT AND PEPPER

To make the remoulade, combine mayonnaise, shallots, capers, mustard, lemon juice, salt and pepper. Stir with a whisk.

SALMON IN PAPILLOTE

SERVES 4 | PREP TIME: 30 MINUTES | COOK TIME: 15 MINUTES

2 TBSP EXTRA VIRGIN OLIVE OIL

1 MEDIUM CARROT, PEELED AND JULIENNED

1 MEDIUM LEEK, WHITE AND LIGHT GREEN PARTS ONLY, CLEANED AND JULIENNED

4 MEDIUM MUSHROOMS, CLEANED AND JULIENNED

4 SMALL SPRIGS TARRAGON

4 THIN LEMON SLICES

1 LB FRESH SALMON FILETS, CUT INTO FOUR EQUAL PORTIONS

4 TBSP WHITE WINE

4 PIECES PARCHMENT PAPER, CUT INTO 14 INCH SQUARES. FOLD PARCHMENT IN HALF AND CUT INTO HEART SHAPES.

Preheat oven to 425°F.

In a small pan of boiling water, blanch the carrot and the leek. Immediately plunge into ice water to stop the cooking.

Open the parchment hearts and brush or spray with olive oil. Place one salmon filet in each heart placing it near the fold and in the middle of the heart. Divide the carrot, leek, mushrooms and shallots into equal portions and place on top of each of the four filets. Sprinkle each filet with 1 tbsp of white wine. Put a sprig of tarragon on each filet.

Fold the top of the parchment over the salmon until the edges meet. Start at the top of the heart and roll a small section of the edge over on itself, then press flat with your fingernail, making a sharp crease. Continue in this way, a small section at a time around to the opposite side completely sealing the packet. When you press the edges of the paper flat, little pleats will form which not only seal the papillote but look pretty as well. When you reach the bottom of the heart give it a twist to seal.

Place a baking sheet in the preheated oven for 5 minutes. Place the papillotes on the hot sheet. Bake the papillotes for 5 to 7 minutes until the packages puff up. Remove from the oven and place the packets on a plate to serve. The packets can be slit open in the kitchen or at the table for a dramatic effect.

"I learned how to cook in a paper container from Jacques Pépin. I've used it in Australia, Singapore, Louisiana and Texas. It's a surprise every time it's brought to the table. The salmon, complimented by the vegetables and lemon is moist and rich."

WINE PAIRING: South Coast Winery Resort & Spa | Sparkling Pinot Grigio | This sparkling wine has nuances of pears and apples, a touch of tropical fruit and finishes with a crisp acidity.

STIR FRIED FLANK STEAK WITH CHIVE CRÊPES

MAKES 12 CREPES | PREP TIME: 50 MINUTES | COOK TIME: 15 MINUTES

CHIVE CRÊPES

6 EGGS, BEATEN

½ TSP CHILI POWDER

1 TSP CHIVES

1 CUP ALL PURPOSE FLOUR

½ TSP SALT

1 ½ CUPS MILK

3 TBSP VEGETABLE OIL

Continued on page 330

Combine eggs, salt, chili powder, chives and flour. Slowly incorporate the milk until you have a smooth batter. Set the batter to rest for 30 minutes.

Heat a small frying pan and coat it with oil. Pour a small amount of batter into the center of the skillet and with a rotating movement, turn the pan until the batter is spread evenly over the bottom.

Cook the crêpe until the bottom is golden, about 30 seconds. Turn the crêpe and cook the other side for about 30 seconds.

Put the finished crêpe on a parchment lined baking tray and cover with a towel to keep warm.

Continued on page 330.

WINE PAIRING: South Coast Winery Resort & Spa | Ruby Cuvee | This sparkling wine has a deep ruby-red color and nuances of strawberries, raspberries and chocolate. It is finished as an extra-dry it with a crisp acidity.

2 (8 OZ) FLANK STEAKS, CUT AGAINST THE GRAIN INTO ¼ INCH BY 3 INCH PIECES

1 CUP SOY SAUCE

½ CUP RICE WINE

¼ CUP HOISIN SAUCE

4 TSP GARLIC, MINCED

1 TSP BROWN SUGAR

1 ½ CUPS WATER

1 TSP JALAPEÑO, DICED

¼ CUP PEANUT OIL

1 TSP FRESH GINGER, MINCED

1 CUP BEAN SPROUTS

1 CUP SNOW PEAS, JULIENNED

½ CUP CARROT, SHREDDED

1 CUP SHITAKE MUSHROOMS, SLICED

½ CUP HONEY

¼ CUP MUSTARD SEEDS

12 CHIVE CRÊPES

Mix together the soy sauce, rice wine, hoisin sauce, 2 tsp garlic, brown sugar and water. Add the flank steak to the mixture and marinate 30 to 60 minutes.

Remove the steak from the marinade and pat dry. Heat a wok or deep-sided sauté pan and add the peanut oil. Add the flank steak and stir fry until golden brown on the outside and medium-rare in the center.

Add remaining garlic and ginger to the browned steak. Then add the bean sprouts, mushrooms, snow peas and carrots. Stir fry on high heat for about 2 minutes until tender crisp. Remove from heat and reserve.

In a small bowl, combine the honey and mustard seeds.

To finish the dish, brush the inside of each crêpe with the honey mustard mixture. Place some of the meat and vegetables in the center of the crêpe and roll into a cylinder. Serve at once.

"MARINATED IN AN ASIAN STYLE SAUCE AND PAIRED WITH CRÊPES FLECKED WITH GREEN CHIVES, ACCOMPANIED BY LOTS OF VEGETABLES AND BRUSHED WITH HONEY MUSTARD SAUCE, THIS IS A DISH FOR ALL MEALS."

VINDEMIA ESTATE

VISITING VINDEMIA VINEYARD AND WINERY IS A UNIQUE EXPERIENCE WITH A CASUAL SOUTHERN CALIFORNIA FEEL.

Climbing the hill to the open air tasting room, a visitor enters a serene atmosphere with delightful views of vineyards and gardens. The name "Vindemia" is Latin for "seasonal grape gathering." Vindemia Winery produces handcrafted wines from Bordeaux blends that represent some of the best varietals grown in the Temecula Valley. Vindemia is conscientious about using sustainable practices in vineyard management that include natural pest control and conservation of energy and water. Owners David and Gail Bradley keep their vineyard soils as rich as possible in microorganisms by composting, preserving native flora and fauna and by using only mineral oil and sulfur to eliminate mildew on vines.

They produce 1,800 cases of wine each year. They grow and harvest grapes for crafting quality red wines, namely Zinfandel, Cabernet, Bordeaux, Viognier, and Syrah. Vindemia also harvests and presses olive oil from 100 olive trees.

The Bradleys also own California Dreamin' Balloon Adventures, giving hot air balloon flights over the scenic vineyards of the Temecula Wine Country.

VINDEMIA
VINEYARDS & WINERY
2013
ESTATE SYRAH

BAKED BRIE WITH APPLE COMPOTE

MAKES 1 (4 ½ INCH) BRIE | PREP TIME: 10 MINUTES | COOK TIME: 1 HOUR 5 MINUTES

- 1 TBSP BUTTER
- 2 APPLES, PEELED, CORED AND CUT INTO ½ INCH CUBES
- ¼ CUP SUGAR
- ⅛ TSP CINNAMON
- 1 (6 TO 8 OZ) BRIE CHEESE, CHILLED
- 10 INCH ROUND OF PUFF PASTRY, ROLLED TO ¼ INCH THICKNESS
- 1 EGG, BEATEN WITH 1 TBSP WATER
- CRACKERS OR SLICES OF BAGUETTE FOR SERVING

Preheat oven to 375°F.

Melt the butter in a saucepan. Add the apples and sauté until they are tender. Add the sugar and cinnamon and cook, stirring occasionally until most of the liquid has evaporated, about 12 to 15 minutes. Remove from the heat and cool to room temperature.

Line a baking sheet with parchment and place the dough on top. Place the chilled brie cheese in the center of the dough. Spread half of the compote over the top of the cheese.

Fold the dough up over the sides of the cheese, pleating the upper edges to fit snugly around the cheese. Pinch the dough together in the center to seal. Brush the dough evenly with the egg wash.

Bake until the pastry is golden brown all over, about 40 to 45 minutes. Let rest for 5 minutes, then transfer to a platter. Serve with crackers and the remaining compote.

WINE PAIRING: Vindemia Estate | Estate Syrah | Wild black fruit overtones wrapped in a peppery finish.

LEMON CAESAR SALAD WITH SOUTHWESTERN CROUTONS

SERVES 8 | PREP TIME: 25 MINUTES | COOK TIME: 10 MINUTES

DRESSING

1 EGG YOLK

JUICE OF 2 LEMONS

1 TSP WORCHESTERSHIRE SAUCE

1 TSP DIJON MUSTARD

1 DASH HOT SAUCE

1 SMALL CLOVE GARLIC

1 TBSP PARMESAN CHEESE, GRATED

⅛ TSP SALT

1 PINCH PEPPER

½ CUP OLIVE OIL

To make the dressing, in a food processor, combine all ingredients except the olive oil. Puree until smooth.

With the machine running, drizzle in the olive oil until it reaches a creamy texture.

WINE PAIRING: Vindemia Estate | Regatta DeBlanc | Viognier with a touch of Roussane. Dry nose with a sweet finish.

SOUTHWESTERN SPICE RUB

1 CUP KOSHER SALT

1 CUP BROWN SUGAR

1 TBSP CUMIN

1 TBSP CORIANDER

1 TBSP PAPRIKA

1 TBSP ONION POWDER

2 TBSP ANCHO CHILE POWDER

1 TBSP BLACK PEPPER

CROUTONS

1 BAGUETTE, CUT INTO LARGE CUBES

1 CUP BUTTER, MELTED

½ BUNCH ITALIAN PARSLEY, CHOPPED

1 TBSP GARLIC, CHOPPED

2 TBSP SOUTHWESTERN SPICE RUB (MAY SUBSTITUTE TEXAS SEASONING)

SALAD

2 HEADS ROMAINE LETTUCE, OUTER LEAVES REMOVED, AND SLICED INTO RIBBONS

4 TBSP PARMESAN CHEESE

To make the Southwestern Spice Rub, mix all ingredients together and store in an air tight container.

NOTE: For a delicious way to use up the remaining rub, see the Oven Roasted Ribs with Southwestern Spice Rub, recipe on page 356.

To make the croutons, preheat oven to 350°F.

Combine the melted butter with parsley, garlic and seasoning. Pour mixture over the bread cubes and toss to mix evenly. Put the cubes on a baking sheet and bake them for approximately 10 minutes or until lightly crisp and golden brown.

For the salad, toss the lettuce and 4 tbsp of the dressing, mix well. Taste and add more dressing if needed. Toss with the croutons and the Parmesan.

Vitagliano
VINEYARDS & WINERY
2016 MUSCAT CANELLI
CALIFORNIA

VITAGLIANO VINEYARDS AND WINERY

THREE GENERATIONS LATER THE VITAGLIANO LEGACY CONTINUES HERE IN THE TEMECULA VALLEY.

Vitagliano Vineyards and Winery produces Super Tuscan style wines, handcrafted to pair with Italian cuisines. They grow Dolcetto, Cabernet Sauvignon, Pinot Grigio and Muscat Canelli on their 10 acres of rolling hills.

Many years ago, when Guy Vitagliano lived in his native village of Santa Maria, Salina, Italy, he was known as a dynamic and passionate wine lover who had a dream of bringing the rich quality of Italian's wines to America. Three generations later his legacy continues here in the Temecula Valley.

Fulfilling the Vitagliano commitment to quality, they nurture each grape and every bottle, watching over the process from beginning to end.

As a small production winery, their exceptional wines are recognized with the first sip.

VEAL SCALLOPS IN LEMONY SAUCE

SERVES 6 | PREP TIME: 20 MINUTES | COOK TIME: 10 MINUTES

- 6 VEAL SCALLOPS, ABOUT ½ INCH THICK EACH
- 2 EGGS
- SALT AND PEPPER
- 2 CUPS PANKO BREAD CRUMBS
- 2 TBSP BUTTER
- ¼ CUP OLIVE OIL
- 1 CUP CHICKEN STOCK
- 4 TSP WORCESTERSHIRE SAUCE
- JUICE OF ½ LEMON

Flatten the veal scallops with a meat pounder until ¼ inch thick.

Whisk the eggs with a pinch of salt and pepper. Put the bread crumbs in another bowl. Coat the veal scallops well on both sides with the egg and then with the bread crumbs. Press the coating down with the flat of your hand.

In a frying pan over medium heat, melt the butter with the olive oil. Add the veal scallops and cook, turning once and brown well, about 2 minutes on each side. Transfer to a warm platter and keep warm.

Pour off the fat. Add the stock, Worcestershire sauce, lemon juice and pepper to taste to the pan. Stir rapidly over medium heat until the sauce is reduced. Pour the sauce over the veal scallops and serve immediately.

"The tender veal scallops are very easy and quick to prepare and the addition of Worcestershire sauce lends a tangy rich flavor."

WINE PAIRING: Vitagliano Vineyards and Winery | Tempranillo | Flavors of cherry, leather and spice.

APPLE CREAM PIE

SERVES 8 | PREP TIME: 30 MINUTES | COOK TIME: 1 HOUR 5 MINUTES

PÂTE BRISÉE

1 ¼ CUPS ALL PURPOSE FLOUR

8 TBSP SWEET BUTTER, CHILLED AND CUT INTO ¼ INCH BITS

⅛ TSP SALT

3 TBSP ICE WATER

2 CUPS APPLES, CHOPPED

¾ CUP SUGAR

2 TBSP FLOUR

1 CUP SOUR CREAM

1 EGG, BEATEN

½ TSP VANILLA

¼ TSP SALT

CRUMBLE

⅓ CUP SUGAR

1 TSP CINNAMON

⅓ CUP FLOUR

¼ CUP COLD BUTTER, CUT INTO ¼ INCH DICE.

To make the pâte brisée Place flour, butter and salt into the bowl of a food processor. Pulse until the flour mixture is incorporated and resembles corn meal. While motor is running, add ice water. Pulse until the dough collects into a ball in the machine. Pour out onto floured surface and shape into a disk. Wrap in plastic and refrigerate for 30 minutes.

Preheat oven to 350°F.

Roll out the dough to a 12 inch circle. Line a 9 inch pie plate with the dough.

Mix all ingredients together and pour into the pastry-lined pie plate. Bake for 15 minutes, then reduce heat to 325°F and continue baking for 30 minutes. Using strips of foil, cover the pie crust edges to prevent burning.

While the pie is baking, make the crumble by thoroughly combining all the crumble ingredients Top the pie with the crumble and bake for 20 minutes more.

WINE PAIRING: Vitagliano Vineyards and Winery | Muscat Canelli | A lovely wine to pair with desserts with aromas of mandarin orange, honeysuckle, pear and nectarine ending on the palate with a hint of grapefruit.

WIENS FAMILY CELLARS

"WE HAVE A LARGE AND TIGHT-KNIT FAMILY WITH A BROAD RANGE OF TALENTS, ALL CONTRIBUTING TO THE SUCCESS OF OUR BUSINESS."
— Doug Wiens, winemaker and viticulturist, Wiens Family Cellars

Wiens Family Cellars is known for making quality red wines that they call "Big Reds", but also make whites and dessert wines. They produce 9,000 cases a year. Some of their favorites are Refugio Cabernet Sauvignon and Château Grand Rouge, as well as the sparkling Amour de L'Orange.

Brothers Jeff, Dave, Doug, and George Wiens run the operation. They emphasize the importance of making quality wines as the motivation to do their own growing and bottling.

The brothers bought 10 acres of planted chardonnay in Wine Country in 2003 and then opened their Temecula winery tasting room in 2006. The operation is supported by 46 members of the extended Wiens family. It began as a hobby and has grown into a successful family business.

Doug Wiens, the winemaker and viticulturist for Wiens Family Cellars says, "We love spending time together and we have amazing cooperation regardless of whether the gathering is for work or play. We have a large and tight-knit family with a broad range of talents, all contributing to the success of our business. We enjoy good food, the company of friends and fine wines."

They also brew beer at Wiens Brewing Company in Temecula.

WIENS
Family Cellars
2017 BARE-KNUCKLE
PETITE SIRAH

BEEF STEW TUSCAN STYLE

SERVES 8 TO 10 | PREP TIME: 20 MINUTES + 2 HOURS FOR MARINADE | COOK TIME: 2 HOURS 35 MINUTES

1 CUP OLIVE OIL

3 TBSP FRESHLY GROUND PEPPER

3 LB BEEF CHUCK OR BRISKET, TRIMMED AND CUT INTO 2 INCH CUBES

2 CUPS RED WINE

1 MEDIUM ONION, DICED

½ LB PANCETTA, CUT INTO MEDIUM DICE

6 CLOVES GARLIC, FINELY MINCED

1 (28 OZ) CAN OF ITALIAN TOMATOES, STRAINED, RESERVE ¼ CUP OF THE TOMATO JUICE

1 CUP BEEF STOCK

SALT

Combine ¾ cup olive oil and 1 tbsp pepper in a non-reactive container. Add the beef cubes to the marinade. Turn the beef frequently. Refrigerate 2 hours or up to overnight.

Preheat oven to 350°F.

Let the meat come to room temperature. Heat 2 tbsp oil in a heavy sauté pan or casserole. Brown the beef on all sides, being careful not to crowd the meat in the pan. Transfer the meat to a platter. Pour the wine in the pan and deglaze scraping up all the good brown bits.

Add the beef back into the pan with the wine.

Add 2 tbsp oil to a sauté pan. Sauté onions and pancetta together and cook until the onions are translucent and the pancetta is cooked through, about 10 minutes. Add the garlic and remaining 2 tbsp pepper and cook 2 minutes. Add the onion mixture to the pan with the beef.

Pulse the tomatoes in a food processor with the ¼ cup of juice until coarsely chopped. Add the tomatoes and the stock to the pan with the beef. Cover and bring to a boil.

Place the covered pan in the oven. Braise for 2 hours. Remove pan from oven, place on the stove and uncover. Gently boil until the stewing liquids are thickened.

Taste and adjust the seasoning. A braised dish like this is even better the next day.

"Talk about hearty! It takes a while to cook but very little prep time. Add some plain boiled potatoes and fresh green beans to complete the plate."

WINE PAIRING: Wiens Family Cellars | Bare Knuckle Petite Sirah | A hearty red wine with black pepper and blueberry flavors finishing with full bodied tannins.

WARM BRUSSEL SPROUTS AND APPLE SALAD

SERVES 6 | PREP TIME: 10 MINUTES | COOK TIME: 25 MINUTES

- ¼ LB BACON, DICED
- ¾ LB BRUSSELS SPROUTS, TRIMMED AND HALVED
- 2 APPLES, PEELED, CORED AND DICED
- 1 SHALLOT, MINCED
- 2 TBSP SHERRY VINEGAR
- 1 TBSP HONEY
- 2 TBSP OLIVE OIL
- ¼ CUP TOASTED WALNUTS, CHOPPED
- SALT AND PEPPER

Sauté the bacon until crispy. Remove the bacon and set aside.

Add the brussels sprouts and sauté for about 15 minutes until browned and slightly soft.

Add the apples and shallots and continue to cook until the apples are slightly soft, 5 minutes more.

Transfer to a bowl.

Whisk together the olive oil, vinegar, honey and a pinch of salt and pepper.

Pour the vinaigrette over the brussels sprouts and apples and stir in the walnuts. Season to taste with salt and pepper. Serve warm.

WINE PAIRING: Wiens Family Cellars | Vermentino | A handcrafted Italian varietal with flavors of pink grapefruit with a touch of mineral lingering.

WILSON CREEK
Rosé
CALIFORNIA
SPARKLING WINE
ALC. 12.0% BY VOL.

WILSON CREEK WINERY & VINEYARDS

The concept for Wilson Creek Winery & Vineyards came about when Gerry and Rosie Wilson's adult children persuaded them to invest in a wine-making enterprise as a family, wanting to start a fun and inviting family business. In 1996, the family bought land along Wilson Creek in the Temecula Wine Country. The creek was named Wilson Creek a hundred years before the family found Temecula.

Wilsons opened their tasting room in 2000 and their Almond Champagne was a huge success. The first ten cases of Almond Champagne sold in four hours. Their next fifty-five cases sold in a week. They continue to sell Almond Champagne, but also have well-rounded offerings of reds, whites, and other sparkling wines.

Today, the Wilsons own 90 acres and produce over 30,000 cases of wine each year. Wilsons credit vineyard manager Greg Pennyroyal for the tremendous work he has done to produce the high quality of fruit grown through innovative and effective farming.

The Wilsons support local charities and have been honored as Business of the Year several times. The winery is a busy, high energy place with a wedding venue, a picnic area, and Creekside Grille restaurant.

OVEN ROASTED RIBS WITH SOUTHWESTERN SPICE RUB

SERVES 4 | PREP TIME: 10 MINUTES + 30 MINUTES TO LET THE DRY RUB SIT ON THE RIBS | COOK TIME: 1 HOUR 45 MINUTES

2 RACKS BABY BACK RIBS

¼ CUP SOUTHWESTERN SPICE RUB

SOUTHWESTERN SPICE RUB

1 CUP KOSHER SALT

1 CUP BROWN SUGAR

1 TBSP CUMIN

1 TBSP CORIANDER

1 TBSP PAPRIKA

1 TBSP ONION POWDER

2 TBSP ANCHO CHILE POWDER

1 TBSP BLACK PEPPER

Place ribs on a rack over a baking sheet.

Rub both sides of the ribs with the spice mixture. Cover and refrigerate for at least 30 minutes or overnight.

Preheat oven to 400°F.

Cook the ribs until the meat pulls away from the bone, 1 ½ to 2 hours.

Raise the oven temperature to 450°F and cook for 15 minutes more.

To make the Southwestern Spice Rub, mix all ingredients together and store in an air tight container.

"Spareribs with a spicy rub produces a delicious result without the mess of a barbecue. We use this spice rub on all our barbecue meats too."

WINE PAIRING: Wilson Creek Winery & Vineyards | Cinsault | A light bodied red wine with aromas of red currants and warm anise on the nose. Light strawberry and black pepper flavors with soft tannins to finish.

ROASTED FENNEL AND POTATOES

SERVES 6 | PREP TIME: 10 MINUTES | COOK TIME: 30 MINUTES

4 TBSP OLIVE OIL

2 FENNEL BULBS

2 LB SMALL BOILING POTATOES (YUKON GOLD)

SALT AND PEPPER

Heat oven to 375°F.

Peel and slice the potatoes into thin rounds. Halve each fennel bulb and slice horizontally into thin slices, a mandolin works best for this.

Add the fennel slices to the potato slices and toss with the olive oil. Sprinkle with salt and pepper.

Spread the fennel and potato mixture in a shallow casserole.

Bake until the potatoes and fennel begin to brown, 25 to 30 minutes.

"The fennel in this casserole imparts a light summery taste to the potatoes. It goes well with the Oven Roasted Ribs with Southwestern Spice Rub (recipe on page 356) and Tuscan Sea Bass (recipe on page 361)."

TUSCAN SEA BASS

SERVES 6 | PREP TIME: 10 MINUTES | COOK TIME: 20 MINUTES

- 6 (4 OZ) SEA BASS FILETS
- ¼ TSP SALT
- ½ TSP PEPPER
- 2 CUPS FLOUR
- 6 TBSP OLIVE OIL
- 2 CLOVES GARLIC, CHOPPED
- 1 (14 OZ) CAN CRUSHED TOMATOES
- ½ CUP WHITE WINE
- 1 TBSP CHOPPED PARSLEY
- 1 TBSP FRESH BASIL LEAVES, CHOPPED

Season the fish with salt and pepper. Put the flour in a shallow bowl, dredge the fish, shaking off excess flour.

In a skillet, heat 3 tbsp of the olive oil and sauté the fish until golden brown on both sides, about 3 minutes per side. Transfer to a warm platter.

Wipe out the pan and heat the remaining 3 tbsp of oil. Add the garlic, tomatoes, wine and parsley. Cook at low heat for 10 minutes. Add the fish back into the pan, add the chopped basil and heat for 2 to 3 minutes.

Serve right away.

"A simple dish with flavors of Tuscany and delicious when served with pasta, soft polenta as shown, or Roasted Fennel and Potatoes (recipe on page 358)."

WINE PAIRING: Wilson Creek Winery & Vineyards | Roussanne | A light and refreshing wine with foral and herbal tea aromas.

LAVENDER AND LEMON CAKE

SERVES 8 TO10 | PREP TIME: 10 MINUTES | COOK TIME: 1 HOUR

- 3 CUPS CAKE FLOUR
- 1 ½ TSP BAKING POWDER
- 1 TSP BAKING SODA
- 1 TSP SALT
- 1 CUP BUTTER, ROOM TEMPERATURE
- 1 ½ CUPS SUGAR
- 1 TBSP DRIED CULINARY LAVENDER FLOWERS, CHOPPED FINE
- 4 LARGE EGGS, ROOM TEMPERATURE
- ½ TSP LEMON EXTRACT
- 1 CUP PLAIN YOGURT, ROOM TEMPERATURE
- 1 TBSP LEMON ZEST

GLAZE

- 2 TBSP HONEY, WARMED UNTIL RUNNY
- ½ CUP POWDERED SUGAR, SIFTED
- 1 TBSP FRESH LEMON JUICE

Preheat oven to 325°F.

Butter and flour a 10 inch spring form pan and line the bottom with parchment.

In a bowl, mix together the cake flour, baking powder, baking soda and salt and set aside.

In the bowl of an electric mixer fitted with the flat beater, cream the butter and sugar until lemony in color and light and fluffy. Add the eggs, one at a time and then beat in the lemon extract.

Add the flour mixture in three additions to the mixer bowl, alternating with the yogurt. Fold in the lemon zest and the lavender.

Pour the batter into the prepared pan. Bake until the cake begins to pull away from the sides of the pan and a toothpick inserted into the center of the cake comes out clean, about 1 hour.

Let the cake cool in the pan for 15 minutes and then unmold.

Place the cake on a rack over a baking sheet and drizzle the glaze over the warm cake.

To make the glaze, mix the honey and lemon juice with the powdered sugar.

WINE PAIRING: Wilson Creek Winery & Vineyards | Sparkling Rosé Wine | The Sparkling Rosé is a refreshing sparkling wine bursting with aromas and flavors reminiscent of strawberries and melons. It is clean and refreshing with balanced acidity and a rich mouth feel.

RECIPES BY WINERY

INDEX

C

Q

R

S

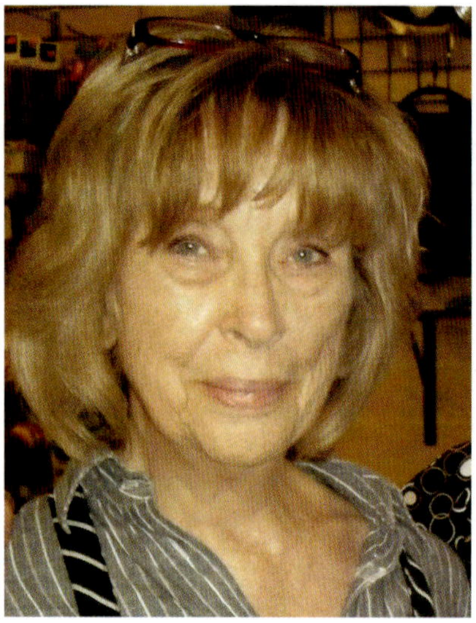

MARTHA CULBERTSON

Martha is a native of San Diego, California, a graduate of SDSU and the Temecula Valley Winegrowers Association 2023 Hall of Fame Inductee. Her McDonald relatives were in agriculture and farming fostering a love of fresh food and inspired by frequent family gatherings for 'farm to table" before that was even an event.

After graduation, she taught school for two years and then joined her Navy diver husband on a tour of duty on the island of Kwajalein. Living in a remote place with little fresh food cemented a belief that fresh, tasty and healthy meals contributed tremendously to a persons' well-being.

Pursuing a career as a commercial diver by John Culbertson meant that the family, which now included sons John and Scott, would be living in Australia and later, spend several years in Singapore. Martha embraced the beautiful seafood of Australia and living in the multi-cultural environment of Singapore opened the door to experience Chinese, Indian and Malay food. She and her husband began to drink wine with dinner enjoying the wonderful vintages of Australia and in Singapore getting to know excellent wines from France.

Returning to America after being "expats" Martha began to study with the great teachers: Julia Child, Jacques Pepin and Diana Kennedy. She went to Italy to study with Lorenza di Medici, and France to study with Simone Beck and was privileged to stay in Julia Child's house, "La Pitchoune" while there. She and her husband traveled extensively in France seeking out the great three star restaurants and those lesser known using the Guide Michelin to point the way.

The Culbertsons went home to California and established a champagne winery with an award winning restaurant. Culbertson Winery was acknowledged as the top award winning winery for several years making methode champenoise. The Temecula wineries were working hard to establish recognition nationally and Martha served on the national Board of Directors of the American Institute of Wine and Food whose board members included Julia Child, Robert Mondavi and Richard Graff. Events held at the winery attracted many luminaries in the culinary world and Culbertson Winery was chosen to represent the American wine industry on a Presidential Trade Mission to Japan. John and Martha accompanied Secretary of Commerce William Verity to Tokyo traveling on Air Force One.

Martha, wanting to share the knowledge, joy and experiences began teaching cooking classes for the local college. The classes were very successful and many of the recipes for this book were developed for those classes. The wine pairings were chosen to enhance the food and celebrate the wine makers.

The cooking classes were produced for over a decade with the help of these women: Deborah Christensen, Carol Steele, Jackie Brown, Kathy Finnell, Susie Bonney, Brittany Tom, Sophia Garcia, Marsha Weaver. A special thanks to Danielle Sergi, Jean Vesey, Karen Fetteroll and Ginger Greaves for their enthusiastic support.

Recipes in this book feature home cooking using French techniques. As Julia Child would say,

"BON APPETIT" AND "BONNE CHANCE."

303
JK-2054

Top Left: Martha Culbertson with her cousin Rod McDonald, Temecula, California, 1978. Bottom Left: Sam Lombardo and John Culbertson, Temecula, California, 1978. Right: Julia Child and Martha Culbertson at Martha's home in Fallbrook, California, 1986.

REBECCA FARNBACH

When Martha Culbertson invited me to coauthor Flavors of the Temecula Valley Wineries, I accepted the challenge immediately knowing that Martha is a talented writer with many stories to share. It has been a good cooperative effort to present the Temecula Valley wineries along with Martha's marvelous recipes paired with Temecula wines.

Martha had conceptualized the book and when I suggested offering it to our newest local publisher, Great Oak Press, we received an enthusiastic response. Besides offering us a contract for Flavors, Great Oak Press also requested that we do a companion book of photographs of our beautiful Wine Country, Portraits of the Temecula Valley Wineries. We accepted the second contract without hesitation.

Wednesdays became our cooking days in Martha's home with Jean Vesey assisting in the kitchen. Martha and Jean prepared five to six delectable dishes each week that were photographed by Johnny Velasquez and sampled by all. I set up photography appointments and interviews on other days at each of the wineries we feature in our books. It was a fun and exciting time for us.

There are many warm and wonderful people working in our wineries and there are so many different winery experiences offered in our area. We truly enjoyed meeting the people of the wine country who opened their hearts to share their stories and give us the feel for the unique places where they ply their trade.

Knowing Martha has given me a new appreciation for food. I grew up in central Iowa, in America's heartland, where our diets were predictable and rather bland. Although I have traveled and eagerly tried new cuisines, Martha has introduced me to flavors, textures and visually pleasing presentations that have gone beyond anything I had known before. Now our readers can see and taste for themselves.

I contributed information about the history of the wineries and the wine country to the two books, formed from personal research and interviews. One of my favorite things is to spend time with people and to listen to their stories, then I interpret their legacies onto pages for others to savor.

My story is that I've written most of my life. Although I can entertain, inform and inspire a crowd from the podium, I am at heart a listener and a reader. I like to see words instead of hearing or speaking them. When I was four years old it disturbed me that I couldn't decipher the written word and I felt a great relief when I finally learned to read.

I read every book in my parents' home, and there were a lot of them. I went to the library to fuel my mind, sometimes waiting outside for someone to exit and open the door because it was too heavy for me.

I like to gather information and then to give it to someone who needs it. My husband Darell and I did a lot of research on the history of Temecula while we championed the preservation of the historic Vail Ranch. We gleaned so much material that it formed the basis for six books I coauthored on the history of the greater Temecula area, including Images of America: Temecula Wine Country.

I first published poetry in my hometown newspaper and co-edited my junior high school newspaper. My first big publication was in Seventeen magazine when I was seventeen years old. I also wrote a recipe pamphlet for the Federal WIC (Women Infant Child) nutrition program that was distributed nationwide in English and Spanish. I am a member of the San Diego Christian Writers Guild. They have granted me several awards, including Writer of the Year in 2005. I have received several other awards for poetry from other groups.

In 1998 I started a writers' critique group where we share our work in progress to give and receive helpful feedback from each other. Each of us benefit from this exercise. The group has published over 130 books so far and our skills are improving. I rejoice with each book produced by our authors.

These books on the Temecula Wine Country are written with love for the region where we live and the people who live and work here. We are blessed to live in the Temecula Valley and appreciate the opportunity to share a glimpse and taste of it with others.

HAPPY READING AND COOKING! — Rebecca Marshall Farnbach

JEAN VESEY

Jean, after winning first place at her high school bake-off, vowed to learn all she could about cooking, baking and grilling. She discovered that a meal is not a refueling stop but a celebration for family and friends.

Performing as one of Martha's assistants for twelve years has taught her how to apply the culinary arts with technical expertise to create inspired dishes.